Morality: A Quranic Perspective

Morality: A Quranic Perspective

Grand Ayatullah Naser Makārem Shirazi

Edited by
Dr. Seyyed Mohsen Miri

Copyright © 2020 Al-Mustafa International Research Institute

All rights reserved. No part of this publication may be reproduced, distributed, or transmitted in any form or by any means, including photocopying, recording, or other electronic or mechanical methods, without the prior written permission of the publisher, except in the case of brief quotations embodied in critical reviews and certain other noncommercial uses permitted by copyright law. For permission requests, write to the publisher, addressed "Attention: - Permissions [Moral Verses]," at the email address below.

Lantern Publications
info@lanternpublications.com
www.lanternpublications.com

All moral rights of the translator and authors have been met.

Ordering Information:
Quantity sales. Special discounts are available on quantity purchases by corporations, associations, and others. For details, contact the distributor at the address below.

Shia Books Australia
www.shiabooks.com.au
info@shiabooks.com.au

ISBN- 978-0-6489869-4-2

First Edition

Content

Content V
Transliteration VIII
Prayers of God's Peace and Blessings IX
Foreword X

Part One: General Moral Problems 1

The Importance of Moral Discussions 2
The Role of Morality in Life 4
Moral Supports 6
Independence of God from Our Moral *Jihad* (Divine War)
.... 7
Is a Master of Morality Required at Any Stage? 9
Predispositions Required for the Cultivation of the Moral Virtues 11
   1. Pure Surroundings 12
   2. The Effect of Companions and Friends 14
   3. The Effect of Family Upbringing 15
   4. The Effect of Science and Knowledge on Upbringing
.... 17
   5. The Effect of Culture of Society 18
   6. The Relationship between Morality and Deeds ... 20
   7. The Relationship between Morality and Eating of the Good Things 21
Practical Steps towards Moral Purification 23
   1. Repentance 24
     A) The Necessity of Repentance 24

B) Repentance and Righteous Deed 26
　　C. The Outcomes and Blessings of Repentance 27
　2. Pledge (*Mushārata*) 29
　3. Divine Meditation (*Muraqaba*) 31
　4. Self-accounting (*Muhāsaba*) 33
　5. Self-reproach (*mu'ātaba*) and Self-punishment (*mu'āqaba*) 35
　　　Sincerity 37
　　　Hypocrisy 38
　　　　How to Overcome Hypocrisy 40
　　　Silence 42
　　　Language 44
　　　Knowledge of the Soul and Knowledge of Allah ﷻ . 46
　　　　A) The Relationship between Knowledge of the Soul and Soul Purification 46
　　　　B) Knowledge of the Soul as a Means of Knowledge of Allah ﷻ 48
　　　Worship and Breeding the Soul 50
　　　Remembrance of Allah ﷻ and Breeding the Soul 52
　　　　The Quality of Remembrance 53
　　　　Impediments of Remembrance 56
　　　Role Models and Exemplars 58

Part Two: Details of Moral Problems 62

Pride and Arrogance 63
Humility and Modesty 65
Greed and Low Temper 67
The Love of the World 68
Envy 70
Pride and Selfishness 72
Long-term Ambitions 73
Fear God 74
Trust 76
Appetites Desire 77

Chastity and Fervor 79
Negligence 81
Stinginess 84
Munificence and Generosity 86
Hurry and Haste 88
Patience 89
Ambition 91
Obstinacy and Making Excuses 93
Thanksgiving 95
Ingratitude 96
Gentleness and Harshness 98
Trusteeship 100
Truthfulness 102
Lie 104
Fulfillment the Covenants 106
Logical Argument and Dispute 108
Reconciliation between People 110
Excuse the Faults and Anger 112
Conciliation and Revenge 113
Suspicion, Spying and Backbiting 115
Suspicion 115
Spying 116
Backbiting 117
Socialism and Isolationism 119

Index 122

Transliteration

Symbol	Transliteration	Symbol	Transliteration
ء	ʾ	أ	a
ب	b	ت	t
ث	th	ج	j
ح	ḥ	خ	kh
د	d	ذ	dh
ر	r	ز	z
س	s	ش	sh
ص	ṣ	ض	ḍ
ط	ṭ	ظ	ẓ
ع	ʿ	غ	gh
ف	f	ق	q
ك	k	ل	l
م	m	ن	n
ه	h	و	w
ي	y	ة	ah
Long Vowels		Short Vowels	
آ	a	◌َ	a
اي	ī	◌ِ	i
او	ū	◌ُ	u
Persian Letters			
Symbol	Transliteration	Symbol	Transliteration
پ	p	چ	ch
ژ	zh	گ	g

At the end of Farsi words, 'eh', '-e', and '-ye' have been used.

Prayers of God's Peace and Blessings

In keeping with the Islamic practice of showing respect for the name of God , and sending prayers of God's peace and blessings whenever the name of His blessed Prophet, Lady Fātema, and the Twelve Imams is mentioned, one or more of the following Arabic symbols have been employed throughout the text. They are repeated for their great rewards.

 Used exclusively after the name of God, meaning "the Sublimely Exalted", or, as a prayer, "[May His name be] Sublimely Exalted".

 Used exclusively after the name of the Prophet, meaning "May the peace and blessings of God be unto him and unto [the purified and inerrant members of] his family"

 Used for any of the Twelve Imams or past prophets of God , meaning "May God's peace be unto him".

 Used for two or more of the Twelve Imams or past prophets of God, meaning "May God's peace be unto them".

 Used for a plurality of the Fourteen Immaculates, meaning "May God's peace be unto them all collectively".

Foreword

Direct and unveiled encountering the reality and truth is one of man's most fundamental rights of which no authority can deprive man. The application of this right opens new horizons to man, prepares the ground for logical and sound cooperation between man on the one hand and man, society, nature, and God on the other, and results in a thorough and moderate growth of man and human values.

However, the way of attaining the truth and reality is not that simple. History bears evidence of this fact, for there has always been some voluntary and involuntary obstacles to man's attaining such a goal. Unfortunately, such obstacles have become more complicated, influential, and widespread in modern times.

One of the realities and truths which has always been a victim of such obstacles is Islam. Ironically, what makes the situation more painful is that despite man's new communicational inventions and achievements that make ways of attaining truths easier, man's attaining Islam's reality has become more difficult. Enemies of Islam have made every effort to draw an unreal and fearful picture of this great religion for non-Muslims of the entire world in the general and western world, particularly in recent decades.

A significant reason for such determined, unprecedented efforts is that the so-called "superpowers" have realized that Islamic teachings can stand against their unlimited greed for rapacity and sucking wealth and blood of the oppressed. That is why they made every direct and indirect effort to cause hatred against Islam since they showed it to be a horrible religion so that they may prevent truth-seekers from embracing it. On the one hand, they have introduced perspectives that have no relation with the true Islam. On the other hand, they have introduced some people they have raised themselves or have indirectly supported who have nothing to do with Islam, such as terrorists and intimidators, as Islam representatives.

A survey of motivations of such efforts can manifest some terrible truths of the satanic plans of enemies of Islam. However, this is something else which should be dealt with in another situation. In this regard, the responsibility of cultural institutes is to prepare the ground for the familiarity of all people who are in search for the truth and cultural development in the entire world with the reality of Islam directly without being influenced by western media or ideologies. Doubtless, knowledge of invaluable human, ethical, and axiological teachings of the Holy Qur'an and those of the Holy Prophet can prepare the ground for the inclination of truth-seekers towards this perfect symbol of truth, i.e., Islam, as it guided so many great thinkers to the truth in the past.

In this connection, Al-Mustafa International Research Institute (M.I.R.I.) attempts to establish a relation between English speaking readers and Islamic truths through preparing simple, conceivable texts so that it may prepare the ground for their fair judgment on Islam. It is hoped that readers' fair reflection could help them overcome obstacles to attaining the truth and remove incorrect images attributed unfairly to Islam so that they may become capable of judging Islam fairly.

FOREWORD

One of these works is the present book entitled *Qur'anic Verses On Moral Values* which includes some verses of the Holy Qur'an and a summary of their commentaries. Extracted from a precious work, *Akhlaq dar Quran* authored by Grand Ayatullah Naser Makarem Shirazi (Imam Ali ﷺ Publication, Qum, 2006, 3 volumes), the present book is applicable in different aspects of life. Seyyed Hossein Hashemiyan and Ali Asghar Hemmatiyan did the extraction of the book published in Persian (*Ayat-e Akhlaqi*, Imam Ali ﷺ Publication Qum, 2014).

Dr. Farideh Amirfarhangi conducted the book's translation and scholarly revision of the English text was done by Dr. Seyyed Mohsen Miri and copy editing by Dr. Abidali Mohamedali.

We hope that this book would be invaluable to the Islamic thought and of great benefit for all readers in general and researchers in particular.

Al-Mustafa International Research Institute (M.I.R.I.)

Part One: General Moral Problems

The Importance of Moral Discussions

لَقَدْ مَنَّ اللَّهُ عَلَى الْمُؤْمِنِينَ إِذْ بَعَثَ فِيهِمْ رَسُولًا مِنْ أَنْفُسِهِمْ يَتْلُو عَلَيْهِمْ آيَاتِهِ وَيُزَكِّيهِمْ وَيُعَلِّمُهُمُ الْكِتَابَ وَالْحِكْمَةَ وَإِنْ كَانُوا مِنْ قَبْلُ لَفِي ضَلَالٍ مُبِينٍ.

Allah certainly favored the faithful when He raised up among them an apostle from among themselves to recite to them His signs and to purify them, and to teach them the Book and wisdom, and earlier they had indeed been in manifest error (3:164).

Summary of Commentary:

One of the main purposes behind the mission of the Prophet ﷺ was the purification of souls, educating human beings, and training in good morals. Even the recitation of the divine verses and the Book and wisdom teachings are an introduction for the purification of souls and training human beings as the primary purposes of the science of morality.

Perhaps this is why "purification" surpasses "education" because the ultimate goal is "purification", although in practice, "education" takes priority over it. In another verse[1], "education" is before the "purification of morality", it overlooks the natural and

---

1. (1: 129). "Our Lord! and raise up in them an Apostle from among them who shall recite to them Thy communications and teach them the Book and the wisdom, and purify them; surely Thou art the Mighty, the Wise."

external order of the issue, where "education" is usually an introduction for the "purification"; therefore, each of the verses considers one aspect of the issue.

Another possibility regarding the purpose of this priority and inferiority is that "education" and "purification" are mutually interactive; that is, as the right training increases the level of morality and the purification of souls, man's moral virtues enhance the level of his knowledge. Man can come to the truth of science when he is free of obstinacy, arrogance, selfishness, and blind bias that hinders scientific progress. Otherwise, such moral defects are a veil over his eyes and heart to find out the truth as it is and naturally cease him to accept it.

The extraordinary effort of the Holy Qur'an to address the moral problems and the purification of souls as a fundamental issue can be referred in many verses. This verse considers the Prophet's mission ﷺ, who is the moral leader and the teacher of the Book and wisdom, as a great grace and the blessing of God, which is due to the importance of morality.

The Role of Morality in Life

وَلَا تَسْتَوِى الْحَسَنَةُ وَلَا السَّيِّئَةُ ادْفَعْ بِالَّتِى هِىَ أَحْسَنُ فَإِذَا الَّذِى بَيْنَكَ وَبَيْنَهُ عَدَاوَةٌ كَأَنَّهُ وَلِىٌّ حَمِيمٌ. وَمَا يُلَقَّاهَا إِلَّا الَّذِينَ صَبَرُوا وَمَا يُلَقَّاهَا إِلَّا ذُو حَظٍّ عَظِيمٍ.

Good and evil [conduct] are not equal. Repel [evil] with what is best. [If you do so,] behold, he between whom and you was enmity, will be as though he were a sympathetic friend. But none is granted it except those who are patient, and none is granted it except the greatly endowed (41: 34-35).

Summary of Commentary:

In this verse, God the Almighty presents a very effective and essential way to terminate malice and hostility. In the first verse, He clarifies morality's role in removing hatred and says, "Repel [evil] with what is best. [If you do so,] behold, he between whom and you was enmity, will be as though he were a sympathetic friend."

Then, in the next verse, He adds that this is not a worthless task, and everybody does not enjoy this kindness and tolerance, "But none is granted it except those who are patient, and none is granted it except the greatly endowed."

One of the most significant problems of human beings' societies is always the accumulation of hatred and hostilities. When they reach their peak, the fire of war sparks destroys everything and turns all into ashes.

Now, suppose the divine method (repelling evil with good) is put into practice. In that case, hatred will disappear as the snow melts in the summer, it will protect societies from the danger of many wars, diminish crimes, and pave the way for public cooperation. However, as the Qur'an says, "None is granted it except those who are patient, and none is granted it except the greatly endowed."

If violence is responded to violently and if another sin repels a sin, violence will exponentially rise. Its scope will be more comprehensive day by day, causing immense misery in society.

Repelling evil with good has certain conditions and exceptions that should be considered.

Moral Supports

يَا أَيُّهَا الَّذِينَ آمَنُوا لَا تَتَّبِعُوا خُطُوَاتِ الشَّيْطَانِ وَمَنْ يَتَّبِعْ خُطُوَاتِ الشَّيْطَانِ فَإِنَّهُ يَأْمُرُ بِالْفَحْشَاءِ وَالْمُنْكَرِ وَلَوْلَا فَضْلُ اللَّهِ عَلَيْكُمْ وَرَحْمَتُهُ مَا زَكَى مِنْكُمْ مِنْ أَحَدٍ أَبَدًا وَلَكِنَّ اللَّهَ يُزَكِّي مَنْ يَشَاءُ وَاللَّهُ سَمِيعٌ عَلِيمٌ.

O, you who have faith! Do not follow in Satan's steps. Whoever follows in Satan's steps [should know that] he indeed prompts [you to commit] indecent acts and wrong. Were it not for Allah's grace and His mercy upon you, not one of you would ever be pure. But Allah purifies whomever He wishes, and Allah is all-hearing, all-knowing (24: 21).

Summary of Commentary:

According to this verse, purity of morality and practice, and complete purification of man are not possible except by divine bounty and mercy. The same meaning is seen with another interpretation in Sura al-A'lā: "Felicitous is he who purifies himself, celebrates the Name of his Lord, and prays." (87: 14-15).

According to these verses, moral and practical purification has a close relationship with the name of the Lord and His prayers and benediction; if purification is derived from the name of the Lord and His prayers, it will be deep and long-lived; but if it is based on other principles, it will be loose and insignificant.

Independence of God from Our Moral *Jihad* (Divine War)

وَمَن جَاهَدَ فَإِنَّمَا يُجَاهِدُ لِنَفْسِهِ إِنَّ اللَّهَ لَغَنِيٌّ عَنِ الْعَالَمِينَ.

Whoever strives, strives only for his own sake. Indeed Allah has no need of the creatures (29:6).

Summary of Commentary:

The purification of the soul is a kind of *jihad* and a struggle with inner enemies [malice, jealousy, pride, etc.] that can destroy human beings.

The Prophet ﷺ sent a group of the warriors of Islam to the *jihad* field; when they returned, he said, "Good for those who carried out *al-jihad al-Asghar*, who should do *al-jihad al-Akbar* as well". Someone asked, "O, the Messenger of Allah ﷺ, what is *al-jihad al-Akbar*?" The Prophet ﷺ replied, "It is the *Jihad* with the soul."[1]

Some verses of the Qur'an regarding *jihad*, are also interpreted about *al-jihad al-Akbar*, in the sense that they are in particular about the *jihad* with the soul, or they refer to a general concept that includes both kinds of *Jihad*.

Regarding this verse (29:6), Tafsir Qumi reads that by *jihad* it means to fight with the soul against the illegitimate lusts,

---

1. *Wasā'il al-Shī'a*, vol.11, p.22 (The first chapter, al-*Jihad al-Nafs*).

pleasures, and sins.[1]

Based on this commentary, jihad is useful for humankind, correct jihad with the soul in this verse.

The last verse of Sura al-'Ankabūt reads: "As for those who strive in Us, We shall surely guide them in Our ways, and Allah is indeed with the virtuous." (29:69)

The phrases "in Us" and "We shall surely guide them in Our ways" in this verse also focus more closely on *al-jihad al-Akbar* or they refer to a general concept that includes both kinds of *jihad*.

---

1. *Tafsir Qumi*, vol.2, p.148; *Biḥār al-Anwār*, vol.76, p.65.

Morality: A Quranic Perspective

Is a Master of Morality Required at Any Stage?

وَمَا أَرْسَلْنَا قَبْلَكَ إِلَّا رِجَالًا نُوحِي إِلَيْهِمْ فَاسْأَلُوا أَهْلَ الذِّكْرِ إِنْ كُنْتُمْ لَا تَعْلَمُونَ.

We did not send [any apostles] before you except as men, to whom We revealed. Ask the People of the Reminder if you do not know (21:7).

Summary of Commentary:

Many mystical wayfaring (*Seyr-u Suluk*) scholars are of the opinion that the followers of the paths of perfection, virtue, and proximity to God (*Qurb-e-Elahi*) should be supervised by a relevant master; however, intellectuals warn that those who wish to attain virtue and the purification of the soul should not easily follow anybody. They should not obey others without sufficiently testing them and being aware of their scientific and religious qualifications.

Anyway, regarding the necessity of choosing a master or a guide, the sentence "Ask the People of the Reminder if you do not know" is sometimes referred to education but not training, since the latter is reliant on the former in many cases; one should certainly get help from the intellectuals, and this meaning is clearly different from the choice of a particular person to monitor his actions and morality. 'Āllama Majlisi narrates a *hadith* in *Biḥār al-Anwār* from Imām 'Alī ibn al- Ḥusayn ﷺ who says,

IS A MASTER OF MORALITY REQUIRED AT ANY STAGE

"Someone who is not guided by a scientist or a wise man will be destroyed!"[1]

However, based on those mentioned earlier, it is not inferred that a private guide is always required to navigate moral problems, so that the program for the purification of morality and piety, and the continuation of mystical wayfaring (*Seyr-u Suluk*) will be disrupted without him. In fact, many figures have referred to the verses of the Qur'an, the Islamic traditions, and the words of the intellectuals in books regarding morality, who have practically practiced them and eventually have attained significant relevant positions. However, nobody can deny that the presence of a private guide and the help of sacred individuals to achieve perfection is the shortest path to achieve moral perfection.

We warn all those who follow this way that if they would like to choose guides for the moral problems, they should take a very cautious approach and be rigorous and accurate in their choice, they should never act based on appearance, they should concern a given guide's background and make such choices in consultation with the intellectuals to achieve their goals.

---

1. *Biḥār al-Anwār*, vol.75, p.159.

Predispositions Required for the Cultivation of the Moral Virtues

To attain moral virtues, the Holy Qur'an discusses seven prerequisites which include:

1. Pure Surroundings
2. The Effect of Companions and Friends
3. The Effect of Family Upbringing
4. The Effect of Science and Knowledge on Upbringing
5. The Effect of Culture of Society
6. The Relationship between Morality and Deeds
7. The Relationship between Morality and Eating of Good Things

PREDISPOSITIONS REQUIRED FOR MORAL VIRTUES

1. Pure Surroundings

وَالْبَلَدُ الطَّيِّبُ يَخْرُجُ نَبَاتُهُ بِإِذْنِ رَبِّهِ وَالَّذِي خَبُثَ لَا يَخْرُجُ إِلَّا نَكِدًا كَذَلِكَ نُصَرِّفُ الْآيَاتِ لِقَوْمٍ يَشْكُرُونَ.

The good land—its vegetation comes out by the permission of its Lord, and as for that which is bad, it does not come out except sparsely. Thus do We paraphrase the signs variously for a people who give thanks (7: 58).

Summary of Commentary:

In this verse, the influence of surrounding man's deeds is delicately expressed. Several great commentators suggest different interpretations of this verse.

Some argue that, like the raindrops, revelation is internalized in individuals' hearts; the virtuous hearts accept it, produce knowledge, and follow piety and obedience as its pleasant outcomes, whereas the sinful hearts do not react appropriately. Therefore, all people's reactions to the invitation of the Prophet ﷺ and the teachings of Islam are not the same, this is not due to a defect in the message, rather a problem in their ability to do their duties.

The second interpretation is that this example tries to confirm that one should always seek goodness and kindness from their proper resources because the effort at inappropriate cases is nothing except for wasting power and energy.[1]

The third possibility in interpreting this verse, which can be used for the present discussion, is that human beings are likened to plants and their living environment to fertile and infertile soils. In a polluted environment, it is challenging to cultivate virtuous human beings despite practical training. Likewise, the life-giving raindrops can never germinate vegetation in infertile soils. For this reason, to purify the soul and enhance righteous morality, it is essential to improve the surrounding. Of course, there is no conflict between these three interpretations; the above analogy may refer to all of them.

An evil social environment is undoubtedly the enemy of moral virtues, whereas a pure environment provides the best and the most suitable opportunity for the soul's purification.

A well-known *hadith* of the Prophet ﷺ reads that the Prophet ﷺ called his companions and told them, "Avoid the (beautiful) plants grown on trash!" They asked, "O, the Messenger of Allah! Whom do the beautiful plants grown on the trash refer to?" The Prophet ﷺ replied, "A beautiful woman who was nurtured in an evil family (and environment)."[2]

This very illustrative simile refers to the effect of the good and bad environments on man's personality. It is a reference to the inheritance as an underlying factor or both.

---

1. This interpretation is discussed in *Majma' al-Bayan* and *Tafsir al-Jadid* regarding the above verse.
2. *Wasā'il al-Shī'a*, vol.14, p.19, No of *hadith*.7; *Biḥār al-Anwār*, vol.100, p.232, No of *hadith*.10.

2. The Effect of Companions and Friends

وَيَوْمَ يَعَضُّ الظَّالِمُ عَلَى يَدَيْهِ يَقُولُ يَا لَيْتَنِى اتَّخَذْتُ مَعَ الرَّسُولِ سَبِيلا. يَا وَيْلَتَى لَيْتَنِى لَمْ أَتَّخِذْ فُلانًا خَلِيلا. لَقَدْ أَضَلَّنِى عَنِ الذِّكْرِ بَعْدَ إِذْ جَاءَنِى وَكَانَ الشَّيْطَانُ لِلْإِنْسَانِ خَذُولا.

A day when the wrongdoer will bite his hands, saying, 'I wish I had followed the Apostle's way! Woe to me! I wish I had not taken so and so as a friend! Certainly he led me astray from the Reminder after it had come to me, and Satan is a deserter of man (25: 27-29).

Summary of Commentary:

These verses refer to the deep sorrow and regret of the wrongdoers on the Day of Judgment when they feel sorry for choosing evil friends because they consider their misfortune due to their friendship.

On the Day of Resurrection, the wrongdoers will be strongly regretful due to the abandonment of their relationship with the Prophet ﷺ, establishing a relationship with the wicked and immoral individuals, and they will explicitly confess these sinful friends as the main cause of their deviation. They will even consider the effect of their evil friends stronger than the effect of the divine messages (albeit on the wicked men), and it is inferred from the interpretation of the last verse that evil friends are part of the Devil's army, in other words, they are evil humans.

It is noteworthy that, in these verses, God expresses the regret of this group with the phrase "the wrongdoer will bite his hands";

and the last stage is to feel sorry. The wrongdoer will bite his finger in the weaker cases, he will bite back of his hand in a severe stage, and he will bite both hands one after the other in tough stages. In fact, this is a kind of revenge on himself. Why did he neglect himself and create his own misery!

What is inferred from the above verses and some other verses of the Qur'an is that friends and companions have a great effect on man's happiness or misery; they affect not only man's morality and behaviour but also influence the formation of his ideas. In this case, the master of morality must always carefully consider all his disciples; especially in the present era, when the distribution of the means of corruption by the wicked friends is terrible and one of the primary sources of all sorts of deviations.

3. The Effect of Family Upbringing

يَا أَيُّهَا الَّذِينَ آمَنُوا قُوا أَنْفُسَكُمْ وَأَهْلِيكُمْ نَارًا وَقُودُهَا النَّاسُ وَالْحِجَارَةُ عَلَيْهَا مَلَائِكَةٌ غِلَاظٌ شِدَادٌ لَا يَعْصُونَ اللَّهَ مَا أَمَرَهُمْ وَيَفْعَلُونَ مَا يُؤْمَرُونَ.

O you who have faith! Save yourselves and your families from a Fire whose fuel is people and stones, over which are [assigned] angels, severe and mighty, who do not disobey whatever Allah has commanded them, and carry out what they are commanded (66: 6).

Summary of Commentary:

PREDISPOSITIONS REQUIRED FOR MORAL VIRTUES

This verse follows the verses inserted at the beginning of Sura al-Taḥrīm that warns the Prophet's wives ﷺ to be strictly mindful of their actions; then, the verse raises the matter as a general precept and addresses all the believers.

Obviously, the word "Fire" here refers to the Fire of Hell; it will not be possible to escape it except through family upbringing, which will lead man to avoid sins and follow piety and obedience. This verse clarifies both the duty of the head of the family regarding those under his care and the effect of education and training on piety and moral virtues.

This training program is concerned with the first component of the family foundation, namely the marriage, and then continues on from the first moment of the child's birth. It should be followed in all stages through the right planning and with the utmost care.

According to a tradition, when the verse was revealed, one of the Prophet's companions ﷺ asked, "How can we keep our families safe from the Fire of Hell?" The Prophet ﷺ replied, "Enjoin them the good (*Amr bil Ma'ruf*) and forbid them the wrong (*Nahy an al Munkar*). If they accept you, you will save them from the Fire of Hell; otherwise, you have done your duty!"[1]

It is also clear from this verse that enjoining the good (*Amr bil Ma'ruf*) is a way to save the family from the Hellfire and to achieve this purpose one should use all means and consider all practical, psychological, and verbal aspects.

---

1. *Tafsir Nūr al-Thaqalayn*. vol.5, p.372.

4. The Effect of Science and Knowledge on Upbringing

وَقَالَ الَّذِينَ لَا يَعْلَمُونَ لَوْلَا يُكَلِّمُنَا اللهُ أَوْ تَأْتِينَا آيَةٌ كَذَلِكَ قَالَ الَّذِينَ مِنْ قَبْلِهِمْ مِثْلَ قَوْلِهِمْ تَشَابَهَتْ قُلُوبُهُمْ قَدْ بَيَّنَّا الْآيَاتِ لِقَوْمٍ يُوقِنُونَ.

Those who have no knowledge say, 'Why does not Allah speak to us, or come to us a sign?' So said those who were before them, [words] similar to what they say. Alike are their hearts. We have certainly made the signs clear for a people who have certainty (1: 118).

Summary of Commentary:

The history of the Prophets ﷺ is full of the excuses that the ignorant nations had against them. The holy Qur'an repeatedly refers to this issue and occasionally focuses on its relationship with ignorance.

In this verse the reliance on ignorance is introduced as a reason for an excuse, and it indicates that this moral deviation has a close relationship with ignorance, as confirmed by many experiences.

5. The Effect of Culture of Society

وَإِذَا بُشِّرَ أَحَدُهُم بِالْأُنثَىٰ ظَلَّ وَجْهُهُ مُسْوَدًّا وَهُوَ كَظِيمٌ يَتَوَارَىٰ مِنَ الْقَوْمِ مِن سُوءِ مَا بُشِّرَ بِهِ أَيُمْسِكُهُ عَلَىٰ هُونٍ أَمْ يَدُسُّهُ فِى التُّرَابِ أَلَا سَاءَ مَا يَحْكُمُونَ.

When one of them is brought the news of a female [newborn], his face becomes darkened and he chokes with suppressed agony. He hides from the people out of distress at the news he has been brought: shall he retain it in humiliation, or bury it in the ground! Look! Evil is the judgment that they make (16: 58-59).

Summary of Commentary:

This verse refers to the terrible story of burying female newborns in the ground during the era of ignorance for the sake of following a false tradition.

The Arabs in the age of ignorance considered the birth of a female baby as a humiliation for themselves, and whenever one was brought the news of her birth, he was so angry that his face became darkened.

He used to hide for days or weeks, constantly debating whether to accept this disgrace, keep his daughter alive or bury her in the ground and get rid of this sorrow. Undoubtedly, murdering especially killing one's own offspring is the worst and the dirtiest deed, but the false traditions destroyed its nastiness in such a way that it was turned into a virtue and pride.

One of the terrible things inserted in some commentaries

regarding the killing of female newborns is that they were being buried in the graves, sometimes drowned in water, sometimes thrown down from the peak of mountains, and sometimes beheaded.[1]

How do these traditions pave the way for the moral vices in their worst forms, and put the worst wickedness in the ranks of the best virtues? This is another evidence that a nation's culture is one of the most important motivations of a tendency to virtues or vices, and those who would like to fight with moral wickedness must work on the modification of the deviant cultures.

The same meaning can be found in the present era that cultures like the Arab culture in the age of ignorance are the source of various moral vices. For instance, at a global conference on women's rights held recently in Beijing, the capital of China, a large group of the participating countries insisted on including three principles in the conference agenda i.e., the freedom of women's sexual relations, the legitimacy of their homosexuality, and the freedom of abortion which was faced with huge controversy by some Islamic countries including Iran.

Obviously, when the so-called educated representatives of peoples and nations defend such shameful and abhorrent deeds as these particular women's rights and culture is formed on that basis, what moral vices would be shared among those peoples and nations? What vices whose harmful effects are manifested in their moral purification and in their social and economic life?

---

1. *Tafsir Ruh al-Ma`ani.* vol.14, p.154. Regarding verses 58-59 of Sura al-Naḥl.

6. The Relationship between Morality and Deeds

قُلْ هَلْ نُنَبِّئُكُمْ بِالْأَخْسَرِينَ أَعْمَالًا. الَّذِينَ ضَلَّ سَعْيُهُمْ فِى الْحَيَاةِ الدُّنْيَا وَهُمْ يَحْسَبُونَ أَنَّهُمْ يُحْسِنُونَ صُنْعًا.

Say, 'Shall we inform you about the biggest losers in regard to works? those whose endeavor goes awry in the life of the world, while they suppose they are doing good' (18: 103-104).

Summary of Commentary:

This verse discusses the most disadvantaged people who lose the vital capital of their lives such as youth, life, and intellectual and physical powers in false ways, where they think they are doing good and therefore feel pleasant and proud of themselves.

Why are these people so miserable today? It is because of the tendency to wickedness and bad temper, as well as following the soul and selfishness that hinder their wisdom to find the truth. They imagine the facts beyond whatever they are. The result of this misery and wretchedness is the same as what is read in the later verse: "They are the ones who deny the signs of their Lord and the encounter with Him" (18: 105).

In Islamic narrations, there are some commentaries in regard to the interpretation of the verse above, each of them is a typical example of different applications of this verse. It is interpreted as the deniers of Amīr al-Mu'minīn 'Alī ﷺ in some traditions; whereas some narratives interpret it as the Christian monks, the hermit men and women who ignore all the pleasures of the world while they are misled. Also, some traditions interpret it as those who commit the heresy of Islam and Muslims. Some commentaries interpret it as the Kharijites of Nahrawān[1] and some others as those who did the heresy of the Jews and Christians; all these are the ones whose deeds are actually wicked, a sin and a crime while they believed themselves to be right and pious.

7. The Relationship between Morality and Eating of the Good Things

يَا أَيُّهَا الرُّسُلُ كُلُوا مِنَ الطَّيِّبَاتِ وَاعْمَلُوا صَالِحًا إِنِّي بِمَا تَعْمَلُونَ عَلِيمٌ.

O apostles! Eat of the good things and act righteously. Indeed I know best what you do (23: 51).

Summary of Commentary:

Some commentators believe that the consecutive use of these two phrases (eating of the good things and act righteously) is due to the relationship between the two terms. In their view, nutrition is influential on deeds and behaviors. Good food purifies the soul and it is the source of good deeds, whereas forbidden and bad food

---

[1] These were the people Imam 'Ali ﷺ fought against in the battle of Naharwān

PREDISPOSITIONS REQUIRED FOR MORAL VIRTUES

make the soul gloomy and lead to the wicked deeds.[1]

Referring to the relationship between the good deeds and the good food, *Tafsir Rūḥ al-Bayān* states that science and wisdom are made by good food; in addition, love and sympathy are formed by good food. The food can be imagined as a seed and the ideas as its fruit, the food can be considered as a sea and the ideas as its pearls. According to this Tafsir, as far as the raindrops are not clear [pure], the pearl of the sea will not be transparent [pure].

Regarding verse 23:51, *Tafsir 'Ithnā 'Ashari*[2] also refers to the relationship between purity of heart, righteous deeds, and good food.

---

1. *Tafsir Nemooneh.* vol.14, regarding verse 23: 51.
2. *Tafsir 'Ithnā 'Ashari.* vol.9, p.145.

Practical Steps towards Moral Purification

Now that we have discussed the important prerequisites for divine morality, it is important to discuss the steps one must take in achieving moral purification. The verses of the Qur'an outline 5 major practical steps one can take to achieve purification these are:

1) Repentance
   A) The Necessity of Repentance
   B) Repentance and Righteous Deed
   C) The Outcomes and Blessings of Repentance
2) Pledge (*mushārata*)
3) Divine Meditation (*Muraqaba*)
4) Self-accounting (*Muhāsaba*)
5) Self- reproach (*mu'ātaba*) and self-punishment (*mu'āqaba*)

These will be elaborated upon briefly in below.

PRACTICAL STEPS TOWARDS MORAL PURIFICATION

1. Repentance

This step can be disussed with 3 major themes

A) The Necessity of Repentance

$$
\text{يَا أَيُّهَا الَّذِينَ آمَنُوا تُوبُوا إِلَى اللَّهِ تَوْبَةً نَّصُوحًا عَسَى رَبُّكُمْ أَن يُكَفِّرَ عَنكُمْ سَيِّئَاتِكُمْ وَيُدْخِلَكُمْ جَنَّاتٍ تَجْرِي مِن تَحْتِهَا الْأَنْهَارُ يَوْمَ لَا يُخْزِي اللَّهُ النَّبِيَّ وَالَّذِينَ آمَنُوا مَعَهُ نُورُهُمْ يَسْعَى بَيْنَ أَيْدِيهِمْ وَبِأَيْمَانِهِمْ يَقُولُونَ رَبَّنَا أَتْمِمْ لَنَا نُورَنَا وَاغْفِرْ لَنَا إِنَّكَ عَلَى كُلِّ شَيْءٍ قَدِيرٌ}
$$

> O you who have faith! Repent to Allah with sincere repentance! Maybe your Lord will absolve you of your misdeeds and admit you into gardens with streams running in them, on the day when Allah will not let the Prophet down and the faithful who are with him. Their light will move swiftly before them and on their right. They will say, 'Our Lord! Perfect our light for us, and forgive us! Indeed You have power over all things.' (66: 8)

Summary of Commentary:

All the scholars of Islam agree on the necessity of repentance and it is repeatedly discussed in the text of the Holy Qur'an like the aforementioned verse.

Being in the charge to lead the deviant nations, all the divine

Prophets ﷺ invited people to repent at the first step because without repenting and purifying the heart from the sins, there will be no room for monotheism and virtues.

The first words of the great Prophet of God, Hūd ﷺ, was, "O my people! Plead with your Lord for forgiveness, then turn to Him penitently." (11: 52)

Similarly the great Prophet, Ṣāliḥ ﷺ, based his work on repentance and told his people, "So plead with Him for forgiveness, then turn to Him penitently." (11: 61)

In Islamic narrations, an emphasis is also placed on the necessity of repentance, including:

1- In his will, Amīr al-Mu'minīn 'Alī ﷺ writes to his son Imām Ḥasan Al-Mujtabā ﷺ, "If you commit a sin, blow it off as soon as possible!"[1]

Of course, given that the Imām is infallible, the purpose here is to encourage others to repent [or it could refer to *tarkul awla* – minor mistakes that the aimmah were capable of].

2- In a similar *hadith*, Imām Riḍā ﷺ narrates from the Prophet of Islam ﷺ that "Nothing is more beloved by God than a faithful man who repents!"[2]

This interpretation can be a reason for the necessity of repentance because repentance is considered to be the most beloved deed before God. In addition, there is a clear rational reason for the necessity of repentance. According to wisdom, there must be a means of salvation from the punishment of God,

---

1. *Biḥār al-Anwār*, vol.74, p.208.
2. *Mustadrak al-Wasā'il*. vol.12, p. 125.

whether certain or probable. Given that repentance is the best means of salvation, it is compulsory based on wisdom. How are guilty people able to keep safe themselves from God's punishment in the world and the Hereafter while they do not repent?

B) Repentance and Righteous Deed

وَإِنِّي لَغَفَّارٌ لِمَنْ تَابَ وَآمَنَ وَعَمِلَ صَالِحًا ثُمَّ اهْتَدَى.

Indeed I am all-forgiver toward him who repents, becomes faithful and acts righteously, and then follows guidance (20: 82).

Summary of Commentary:

Repentance means to return from God's disobedience to His obedience which results from feeling regretful for the previous deeds; repentance is the need for this regret and knowing that sins hinder man to reach the real beloved (God). The decision to avoid sins in the future means to compensate for the losses; that is, to the extent a wrongdoer is able, he should eliminate the effects of the previous sins from his existence, and if there are compensable rights, he should compensate them. For this reason, many verses of the Holy Qur'an [1] repeat this meaning and mention repentance together with purification and

---

1. (2: 160), (3: 89), (4: 146), (24: 5), (16: 119), (6: 54).

compensation.

In the aforementioned verse, in addition to the returning and righteous act (compensation of the past) as the two pillars of repentance, faith and guidance are also referred to.

In fact, sins weaken faith and deviate man from guidance; for this reason, he must renew his faith after repentance and return to guidance.

According to this verse and the similar ones, the logic of the Qur'an in regard to repentance is quite clear; real repentance is not just verbal forgiveness, repentance from the previous misdeeds, or decision to avoid sins in the future; rather in addition to these efforts, the shortcomings occurred in the past, the corruptions of the soul, and the outcomes of sins in society must be compensated as far as possible and they must be completely removed.

C. The Outcomes and Blessings of Repentance

وَالَّذِينَ لَا يَدْعُونَ مَعَ اللهِ إِلَهًا آخَرَ وَلَا يَقْتُلُونَ النَّفْسَ الَّتِى حَرَّمَ اللهُ إِلَّا بِالْحَقِّ وَلَا يَزْنُونَ وَمَنْ يَفْعَلْ ذَلِكَ يَلْقَ أَثَامًا. يُضَاعَفْ لَهُ الْعَذَابُ يَوْمَ الْقِيَامَةِ وَيَخْلُدْ فِيهِ مُهَانًا. إِلَّا مَنْ تَابَ وَآمَنَ وَعَمِلَ عَمَلًا صَالِحًا فَأُولَئِكَ يُبَدِّلُ اللهُ سَيِّئَاتِهِمْ حَسَنَاتٍ وَكَانَ اللهُ غَفُورًا رَحِيمًا.

Those who do not invoke another god besides Allah, and do not kill a soul [whose life] Allah has made inviolable, except with due cause, and do not commit fornication. (Whoever does that shall encounter its retribution, the punishment being doubled for him on the Day of Resurrection. In it he will abide in humiliation forever, excepting those who repent, attain faith, and act righteously. For such, Allah will replace their misdeeds with good deeds, and Allah is all-forgiving, all-merciful (25: 68-70).

Summary of Commentary:

The blessings and benefits of repentance are abundant which are widely mentioned in verses and narratives. By blessings, it means not only does repentance cover and destroys sins, but also turns them into good deeds, as stated in the verse God says: "excepting those who repent, attain faith, and act righteously. For such, Allah will replace their misdeeds with good deeds." (25: 70)

When repentance is completely pure, God covers the works of the sins so that, as narrated in a *hadith*, even the angels in the charge of registering the wrongdoer's deeds forget everything. God orders the limbs of his body, which are the agents of testifying against his actions on the Day of Judgment, to cover his sins. God also commands the land, in which man committed the sins, to testify against his performance on the Day of Resurrection and conceal his sins so that on that Day, nobody and nothing will testify against him.

Some of the blessings and benefits of repentance are as follows:

- Repentance destroys the sins.[1]
- Repentance blesses the earth and the heaven.[2]

2. Pledge (*Mushārata*)

مِنَ الْمُؤْمِنِينَ رِجَالٌ صَدَقُوا مَا عَاهَدُوا اللَّهَ عَلَيْهِ فَمِنْهُمْ مَنْ قَضَى نَحْبَهُ وَمِنْهُمْ مَنْ يَنْتَظِرُ وَمَا بَدَّلُوا تَبْدِيلًا.

Among the faithful are men who fulfill what they have pledged to Allah. Of them are some who have fulfilled their pledge, and of them are some who still wait, and they have not changed in the least (33: 23).

Summary of Commentary:

According to the great scholars in the field of morality, the first step after repentance is a pledge (*mushārata*), it means man promises to his soul through daily remembrance. The best time for this remembrance is after the morning prayers when he is enlightened by the great divine worship.

He addresses his soul and reminds himself that he has nothing

---

1. (66: 8).
2. (71: 10-12).

except for his precious life, and if it is lost, he will have nothing. Remembering the honorable verse, "By Time! Indeed, man is in loss"(103: 1-2), man reminds his soul that losing this capital means being faced with a huge loss, unless he gets the more precious commodity, the one mentioned in the Sura as follows: "except those who have faith and do righteous deeds, and enjoin one another to [follow] the truth, and enjoin one another to patience." (103:3).

He must remind himself, "Imagine your life is over and you are really sorry for seeing the post-death events and the bitter facts revealed by the removal of the veils and you cry out: "My Lord! Take me back, that I may act righteously in what I have left behind." (23: 100)

Let's assume that you did not get the negative response, "By all means!" Allah accepted your request and today you will return to the world, tell me what you are going to do to compensate for the shortcomings and mistakes of the past! Of some prayers of Imām Sajjād in *Ṣaḥīfa Sajjādiyya*, it is inferred that the great Imām had also a particular interest in the issue of "pledge" (*mushārata*).

In his thirty-first prayer, the famous prayer on repentance, He prays before Allah, "My Lord, I pledge before you I will not repeat whatever you do not like me to do, I guarantee I will not conduct whatever you blame, and I promise I will abstain from all the sins."

It is inferred from the other verses of the Qur'an that the Prophet's companions used to promise Allah in important issues which was in turn a kind of pledge (*mushārata*).

It is stated in the Qur'an that, "Among the faithful are men who fulfill what they have pledged to Allah ﷻ. Of them are some who have fulfilled their pledge (*mushārata*), and of them are some who still wait, and they have not changed in the least." (33: 23)

In short, "pledge" (*mushārata*) is one of the significant steps taken to purify morality; without which, neglect and pride darken man's heart and soul and make it much more difficult for him to save himself.

3. Divine Meditation (*Muraqaba*)

يَا أَيُّهَا الَّذِينَ آمَنُوا اتَّقُوا اللَّهَ وَلْتَنظُرْ نَفْسٌ مَّا قَدَّمَتْ لِغَدٍ وَاتَّقُوا اللَّهَ إِنَّ اللَّهَ خَبِيرٌ بِمَا تَعْمَلُونَ.

O you who have faith! Be wary of Allah, and let every soul consider what it sends ahead for tomorrow, and be wary of Allah. Allah is indeed well aware of what you do (59: 18).

Summary of commentary:

The term "Divine Meditation" (*Muraqaba*) refers to the monitoring, investigation, and observation of something. Based

PRACTICAL STEPS TOWARDS MORAL PURIFICATION

on the commentaries of the scholars of morality, this term is used in regard to "self-care". It is a stage after "pledge" (*mushārata*), that is, a person must be careful of his own purity after his pledge (*mushārata*) with himself to obey the commands of God and avoid sins. This is because if he neglects this, all the pledges will be destroyed.

In fact, a human being in this world is like someone who has precious capital; passing a crowded market, he would like to do the best purchase, while surrounded by thieves and cheats. If he neglects his exquisite capital for a moment, they will plunder it and he will be left alone with a lot of grief and regret. It is precisely the same; jinn and human devils in this world surround man, invite his soul towards themselves. If man does not raise himself up to God and he is not careful of his deeds, his faith and piety will be destroyed and he will move to the Hereafter with bare hands.

God says to the believers, "O you who have faith! Be wary of Allah, and let every soul consider what it sends ahead for tomorrow, and be wary of Allah. Allah is indeed well aware of what you do." (59: 18). In fact, the sentence "and let every soul consider what it sends ahead" refers to "Divine Meditation" (*Muraqaba*).

In a *hadith*, Imām 'Alī ﷺ says, "It is desirable for man to dominate himself, always take care of his heart, and keep his tongue."[1]

---

1. *Ghurar al-Hikam wa Durar al-Kalim*, No of *hadith*, 4732.

In one of his sermons, Imām 'Alī ﷺ says, "May Allah bless anyone who cares for himself (in his deeds), who refrains from the sins, who struggles with his soul, and who denies the dreams."[1]

In short, a follower of the right path and the way of Allah ﷻ must always care for his deeds after the "pledge" (*mushārata*), the promise with himself and his God, to obey Him, purify his soul and not to breach this pledge (*mushārata*); and just like a creditor who asks his allies the money owed to him, he should request his soul to remain loyal to this divine promise.

4. Self-accounting (*Muḥāsaba*)

يَا بُنَيَّ إِنَّهَا إِن تَكُ مِثْقَالَ حَبَّةٍ مِّنْ خَرْدَلٍ فَتَكُن فِي صَخْرَةٍ أَوْ فِي السَّمَاوَاتِ أَوْ فِي الْأَرْضِ يَأْتِ بِهَا اللَّهُ إِنَّ اللَّهَ لَطِيفٌ خَبِيرٌ.

'O my son! Even if it should be the weight of a mustard seed, and [even though] it should be in a rock, or in the heavens, or in the earth, Allah will produce it. Indeed Allah is all-attentive, all-aware.' (31: 16)

Summary of Commentary

---

1. Biḥār al-Anwār, vol.74, p.349.

PRACTICAL STEPS TOWARDS MORAL PURIFICATION

The fourth step that the scholars of morality outline for the followers of the way of Allah is self-accounting; that is, man should audit his performance at the end of every year, every month, every week, or ideally every day. He should account for his good and evil deeds, obedience and sins, as well as theism and following his soul precisely.

Certainly, self-accounting (*Muhāsaba*) of the faith or the world has one of the two most important benefits: if a bill represents a huge profit, it is due to the correctness of the performance, the procedure, and the need to pursue it; while if there is a significant loss, it is because of the existence of a crisis, a danger, and the likelihood of the presence of the cheats, thieves, incognizant ones, and wrongdoers that may be involved and therefor modification is required as soon as possible.

In this regard, there are also meaningful references in Islamic sources, including verses and traditions.

Numerous verses of the Holy Qur'an discuss the exact self-accounting (*Muhāsaba*) on the Day of Judgment; among the verses is verse 16 of Sura Luqmān where Luqmān Hakīm tells his son, 'O my son! Even if it should be the weight of a mustard seed, and [even though] it should be in a rock, or in the heavens, or in the earth, Allah will produce it. Indeed Allah is all-attentive, all-aware.' (31: 16)

The issue is so important that one of the names of the Day of Judgment is "The Day of Reckoning" ("*Yawm Al- Ḥisāb*"), ' indeed those who stray from the way of Allah—there is a severe punishment for them because of their forgetting the Day of Reckoning.' (38: 26)

In Islamic narratives, there are many recommendations regarding reckoning, including a famous *hadith* of the Messenger of Allah who has said, "Account your own performance before your self-accounting [on the day of judegment], weigh your deeds before their weighting! (determine your value before it is determined for you), and prepare yourself for the great presence (the Day of Judgment)". [1]

5. Self-reproach (*mu'ātaba*) and Self-punishment (*mu'āqaba*)

وَلَا أُقْسِمُ بِالنَّفْسِ اللَّوَّامَةِ.

And I swear by the self-blaming soul! (75: 2)

Summary of Commentary:

---

1. *Biḥār al-Anwār*, vol.67, p.73.

PRACTICAL STEPS TOWARDS MORAL PURIFICATION

The fifth step after "self-accounting" (*muḥāsaba*) is self-reproach (*mu'ātaba*) and self-punishment (*mu'āqaba*) of the soul against the previous mistakes and wrongdoings; if man accounts his misdeeds but does not react to them, the result will be reversed; in other words, it will lead to boldness and self-esteem of the soul in wrongdoing.

Just like that, when one calls on ones' employees, workers or partners, to account for their infringements and mistakes, reacts against their misdeeds, and in some ways punishes them through reproaching or various forms of punishment. Those who go along the path of God and are engaged in the purification of their souls, also have to punish their disobedient souls; otherwise, the result of the reckoning will be reversed; that is, it will lead to more courage and impudence.

The Holy Qur'an, to the extent that it matters, swears by the self-blaming soul and says, "And I swear by the self-blaming soul!"

It is clear that the self-reproach (*mu'ātaba*) of the soul is the awakening conscience that reproaches man for wrongdoing which is a kind of self-reproach (*mu'ātaba*) and self-punishment (*mu'āqaba*).

Self-reproach (*mu'ātaba*) and self-punishment (*mu'āqaba*) against the misdeeds has a hierarchy that begins with the reproaching, then it proceeds to more severe stages such as depriving oneself of some of the benefits of living in a certain period.

In Islamic *hadiths*, there are also references to self-punishment (*mu'āqaba*). Among these, Imām 'Alī ؑ describes the outstanding characteristics of a pious individual in *Nahj al-Balāgha* and says, "When his soul disobeys to perform the duties, it would not like to do (and follows the wrong path), he will deprive it of what it would like to do (and thereby he punishes the rebellious soul). [1]

It means, he deprives his disobedience soul of what it desires such as sleep, food, and rest to punish it in such a way that it would no longer like to follow the path of disobedience.

Sincerity

فَادْعُوا اللَّهَ مُخْلِصِينَ لَهُ الدِّينَ وَلَوْ كَرِهَ الْكَافِرُونَ.

So supplicate Allah, putting exclusive faith in Him, though the faithless should be averse. (40:14)

Summary of Commentary:

Sincerity means that the motive for making decisions is only God. There may be those who have a strong will to do what they intend purposes, however their motives to achieve their ends is material; the followers of the path of God are those whose intent is combined with sincerity and originate from the divine motives.

Sincerity is found in the verses of the Holy Qur'an, Islamic narrations and the words of the infallible Imāms who consider sincerity as the main factor of felicity in the world and the

---

1. *Nahj al-Balāghah*. No of *khutbah*, 193.

Hereafter. In principle, in Islam, every action without sincerity is worthless. Various verses of the Qur'an[1] describe those who have exclusive faith in Allah ﷻ and praise these individuals in various and meaningful terms, including the aforementioned verse.

Sincerity is also discussed in several narrations. For instance, Imām 'Alī ؑ says in a *hadith* report, "Blessed is he who makes his worship and prayer exclusive for God, who does not engage his heart in what he sees or does not forget remembrance of God due to what he hears, and who does not experience saddened because of helping the others.[2]

Hypocrisy

إِنَّ الْمُنَافِقِينَ يُخَادِعُونَ اللهَ وَهُوَ خَادِعُهُمْ وَإِذَا قَامُواْ إِلَى الصَّـــلاَةِ قَامُواْ كُسَالَى يُرَآؤُونَ النَّاسَ وَلاَ يَذْكُرُونَ اللهَ إِلاَّ قَلِيلاً.

The hypocrites indeed seek to deceive Allah, but it is He who outwits them. When they stand up for prayer, they stand up lazily, showing off to the people and not remembering Allah except a little (4: 142).

---

1. (98: 5), (39: 11), (15: 39-40), (37: 39, 40, 127, 128, 159, and 160), (12: 24).
2. *Uṣūl al-kāfī*. vol.2, p.16.

Summary of Commentary:

The opposite of "sincerity" is "hypocrisy" which is denounced in the verses of the Qur'an and Islamic narrations. It is introduced as a factor in falsifying acts, as a sign of the hypocrites, and as a kind of polytheism.

Hypocrisy destroys moral virtues; it is a factor in distributing the seed of vices in man's soul. Hypocrisy makes actions worthless and prevents man from addressing the content and truth of the actions.

Hypocrisy is one of the most important tools used by Satan to mislead man.

Several verses of the Qur'an[1] refer to hypocrisy, including the verse above which describes hypocrisy as one of the behaviors of the hypocrites, "The hypocrites indeed seek to deceive Allah, but it is He who outwits them. When they stand up for prayer, they stand up lazily, showing off to the people and not remembering Allah except a little."

It is noteworthy that discord is a kind of dichotomy of appearance and conscience, and hypocrisy is also another form of this dichotomy because the appearance of an action is divine but its inner being is devilish, hypocritical, and to attract people's attention! Therefore, dichotomy is naturally a part of the program of hypocrites.

---

1. (2: 264), (18: 110), (4: 38), (8: 47).

Numerous narrations from our holy aimmah also pay attention to the importance of hypocrisy. For instance, it is reported from the Holy Prophet ﷺ to have said, "On Day of Resurrection, the hypocrite is called and told, 'O the deceiver, O the hypocrite, your actions have been lost and your rewards have been gone away, go and receive your rewards from the one you have acted for."[1]

How to Overcome Hypocrisy

إِن يَنصُرْكُمُ اللّهُ فَلاَ غَالِبَ لَكُمْ وَإِن يَخْذُلْكُمْ فَمَن ذَا الَّذِي يَنصُرُكُم مِّن بَعْدِهِ وَعَلَى اللهِ فَلْيَتَوَكَّلِ الْمُؤْمِنُونَ.

If Allah helps you, no one can overcome you, but if He forsakes you, who will help you after Him? So in Allah let all the faithful put their trust (3: 160).

Summary of Commentary:

To struggle with hypocrisy, just as with all the moral vices, two things should be done: first, to find out its causes and origins to destroy and remove them, and then to consider its outcomes in order to be aware of the painful consequences awaiting those who follow the vice. The root of hypocrisy is the same as the

---

1. *Al - Mahajja al - Baydā'*, vol. 6, p. 141.

"practical polytheism" and the lack of attention to the truth of monotheism. If the foundations of the "practical monotheism" are firmly internalized; if dignity, humility, and blessings are firmly belived to the in the hands of Allah; and if the hearts of the people are at His will and discretion, one can never rely upon his actions on the pleasure of others.

If we know with certainty that the one who is with God has everything, and the one who is detached from Him suffers from the lack of everything, in accordance with the verse above, "If Allah helps you, no one can overcome you, but if He forsakes you, who will help you after Him?"; and if we are certain of the Qur'anic fact that all glory is with God and at His hands as it is read in the verse "Do they seek honor with them? [If so,] indeed all honor belongs to Allah." (4: 139); and if faith in these matters is deeply rooted in the depths of the soul, then there will be no reason for man to destroy his deeds with hypocrisy for the sake of attracting people's attention and enjoying their trust and respect.

Some scholars of morality argue that the basic reason of hypocrisy is ambition which goes back to three principles: the interest in being praised by people, keeping oneself away from people's blame and condemnation, and the greed of what people enjoy.

It is also noteworthy that concealing the impure intentions due to hypocrisy is not possible for extended periods of time. Hypocrites are often recognized and scandalized in this world, they are revealed through their words and behaviors, their infidelity is revealed, and they lose their value in the eyes of people. Attention to this meaning also has a significant inhibitory effect. The pleasure of the pure deed and intent for man is not comparable to anything else and this is enough for the purity of intent.

Some scholars of morality believe that one of the ways to overcome hypocrisy is that man should attempt to hide his worship and good deeds, he should perform acts of worship in solitude, he should try to conceal his good actions to get used to it gradually.

However, this does not mean that one should not participate in the Friday prayers, the Hajj pilgrimage, and other mass activities; in that case, it will be a great loss!

Silence

فَكُلِي وَاشْرَبِي وَقَرِّي عَيْنًا فَإِمَّا تَرَيِنَّ مِنَ الْبَشَرِ أَحَدًا فَقُولِي إِنِّي نَذَرْتُ لِلرَّحْمَنِ صَوْمًا فَلَنْ أُكَلِّمَ الْيَوْمَ إِنسِيًّا.

Eat, drink, and be comforted. Then if you see any human, say, "'Indeed I have vowed a fast to the All-beneficent, so I will not speak to any human today." (19: 26)

Summary of Commentary:

This verse refers to the story of Mary. In the very difficult moments that she was suffering from severe pangs of childbirth that led her to leave her hometown to the desert, she was really doleful as her infant's birth would lead to slander by the disbelievers. So concerned was she that she requested the God take her life; at that time, she heard a voice giving her orders, "The birth pangs brought her to the trunk of a date palm. She said, 'I wish I had died before this and become a forgotten thing, beyond recall.' Thereupon he called her from below her [saying,] 'Do not grieve! Your Lord has made a spring to flow at your feet. Shake the trunk of the palm tree, freshly picked dates will drop upon you. Eat, drink, and be comforted. Then if you see any human, say, "Indeed I have vowed a fast to the All-beneficent, so I will not speak to any human today." ' (19: 23-26)

Whether the voice was Gabriel's or Mary's infant's (that is, Jesus) has led to some discussions among the commentators. However, what we are concerned about here is that the command to vow a silence fast was a divine command, whether by the divine message angel (Gabriel) or by Jesus. The vow is usually given to work that has a divine preference; thus, the "fast of silence", at least, in that nation was a divine act, and the interpretation of the verse suggests that the vow of silence was known to the people of that time; for that reason, when Mary pointed to her silence, nobody objected.

It is also believed that Mary's fast was for the avoidance of drinking water, eating food, and talking to the people but not just for silence.

Of course, the fasting of silence is sanctioned in the Shari'a of Islam because of the difference in the terms of time and place; in some instances it is important to speak up as a *hadith* of Imām Sajjād ﷺ reads that "fast of silence is forbidden."[1]

The significance of "silence" has a great deal of respect and reverence in Islamic narrations. For instance, a *hadith* of Imām Riḍā reads, "silence is one of the doors of knowledge. Silence brings affection, and it is the reason and guidance of all goodness."[2]

Language

وَلَوْ نَشَاءُ لَأَرَيْنَاكَهُمْ فَلَعَرَفْتَهُمْ بِسِيمَاهُمْ وَلَتَعْرِفَنَّهُمْ فِي لَحْنِ الْقَوْلِ وَاللَّهُ يَعْلَمُ أَعْمَالَكُمْ.

If We wish, We will show them to you so that you recognize them by their mark. Yet you will recognize them by their tone of speech, and Allah knows your deeds (47: 30).

Summary of Commentary:
Undoubtedly, language is the gate of man's soul; that is, through

---

1. *Wasā'il al-Shī'a*, vol.7, p.390. Chapter on the sanction of silence fast.
2. *Uṣūl al-kāfī*. vol. 2, p. 113.

the words uttered by a speaker, one can easily understand his or her personality. On the contrary, the words used by the speaker affect his own soul and gradually they change his personality; thus, the two have a mutual effect.

Among the verses of the Holy Qur'an, the aforementioned verse confirms that there is a special relationship between language, intellect, and morality that with regard to the uttered words, one can explore man's soul. This relationship forms the earliest days of ones life and is used to discover the intentions, thoughts and secrets of individuals.

This verse, referring to the hypocrites, says "If We wish, We will show them to you so that you recognize them by their mark. Yet you will recognize them by their tone of speech, and Allah knows your deeds."

According to Rāghib in "*Mufrādī*", "tone" means distorting the talk from its specific rules and traditions, or giving it a wrong pronunciation, or even turning the words from precision into allusion and metaphor. The meaning of the term "tone of speech" in the verse is the last meaning; that is, we can recognize the hypocrites through their two-sided or false interpretations and then we can understand their secrets.

In a *hadith*, Abu Sa'id Khudrī says, "The meaning of 'tone of speech' is the hatred and enmity with Imām 'Alī ﷺ (one of its clear examples is the expression of hostility with that Imām). We can recognize the hypocrites in the age of the Prophet ﷺ from their malice toward Imām 'Alī ﷺ."¹

Knowledge of the Soul and Knowledge of Allah ﷻ

One of the important connections in moral purifications is that of the connection of the soul and the unlimited knowledge of Allah ﷻ. The following verses refer to the this sacred connection.

A) The Relationship between Knowledge of the Soul and Soul Purification

وَلَا تَكُونُوا كَالَّذِينَ نَسُوا اللَّهَ فَأَنسَاهُمْ أَنفُسَهُمْ أُوْلَئِكَ هُمُ الْفَاسِقُونَ.

And do not be like those who forget Allah, so He makes them forget their own souls. It is they who are the transgressors (59: 19).

Summary of Commentary:

How does knowledge of the soul lead to its purification? The reason is clear. First: through knowledge of ones soul, man can find out the dignity of his soul, the greatness of this great divine

---

1. *Majma' al-Bayan fi-Tafsir al- Qur'an.* vol.9, p.106, in regard to the aforementioned verse- The content of this *hadith* is cited by many *Sunni* scholars in their books, including Ahmad Hanbal in "*Fazail*", ibn Abd al-Barr, in "*The Comprehensive Compilation of the Names of the Prophet's Companions*", Zahabi in "*Tarikh al-Islam*", Ibn al-Athir in "*Jami' al-Usul*".

creation, and the importance of his soul that is a part of the divine light and a blow of the divine breath; he can understand that this is like a precious gem that should not be sold at a low price or should not be lost easily.

Second: through knowledge of ones soul, man can be aware of the dangers of the soul, and the motivations of his lust and in general their contradictions with his bliss; thus knowledge of the soul can prepare man to deal with them.

Obviously, someone who does not know his soul is unaware of these motivations and is like someone surrounded by enemies, but he is unaware of their existence. It is natural that such a person is not prepared to confront the enemies, and finally, he is hurt by them.

Third: through knowledge of the soul, man can find out the different talents God provides him for his development and progress, and he is encouraged to cultivate these talents, make them flourished, extract these treasures, and reveal his own essence. Otherwise, he is like a man who lives in his house full of the buried precious treasures, but he is not aware of them; he may die of hunger and poverty, while under his feet there is a hoard of treasure that can feed thousands of people.

Fourth: every moral corruption and vice has roots in the soul of man; through knowledge of the soul, these roots can be discovered, and lead to ease in solving many painful problems; thus, knowledge of the soul will pave the way to refine the soul.

Fifth: most importantly, knowledge of the soul is the best way to attain knowledge of Allah and as it will be discussed, knowledge of Allah and awareness of the qualities of majesty and elegance of Allah are the strongest factors for the cultivation of the moral values, man's perfection, salvation from misdeeds, and attainment of virtues. If this is added to the previous discussion that the moral wrongdoing destroys man's life, hurts the society in severe crises, and turns the nectar of his life into poison, the importance of self-awareness in man's life can be revealed.

Thus, Allah punishes the wrongdoers by making them forget themselves and warns the Muslims, "And do not be like those who forget Allah, so He makes them forget their own souls. It is they who are the transgressors."

In a *hadith*, Imām 'Alī says, "A true mystic is the one who knows himself, frees himself (from the bondage), and purifies his soul from everything that hinders him from achieving bliss."[1]

This interpretation refers to the fact that knowledge of the soul releases man from the bondage and cleans his soul from the moral vices.

B) Knowledge of the Soul as a Means of Knowledge of Allah

سَنُرِيهِمْ آيَاتِنَا فِي الْآفَاقِ وَفِي أَنفُسِهِمْ حَتَّى يَتَبَيَّنَ لَهُمْ أَنَّهُ الْحَقُّ أَوَلَمْ يَكْفِ بِرَبِّكَ أَنَّهُ عَلَى كُلِّ شَيْءٍ شَهِيدٌ

---

1. *Ghurar al-Hikam wa Tabag al-Mizan*. vol.6, p.173.

Soon We shall show them Our signs in the horizons and in their own souls until it becomes clear to them that He is the Real. Is it not sufficient that your Lord is witness to all things? (41: 53)

Summary of Commentary:

In another verse it says, "And in your souls [as well]. Will you not then perceive?" (51: 21)

Some scholars infer from the verse on the Dharr world that knowledge of the soul (*ma'rifat al-nafs*) is the basis of knowledge of Allah (*Ma'rifat Allah*). God says, "When your Lord took from the Children of Adam, from their loins, their descendants and made them bear witness over themselves, [He said to them] 'Am I not your Lord?' They said, 'Yes indeed! We bear witness.'" (7: 172)

Ayatollah Tabatabai in *Tafsir al-Mizan* states that, "No matter how arrogant a person is and how proud he is because of his comfortable rich life, he cannot deny the fact that he is not the owner of his own being, and that he does not have autonomy in his own life; otherwise, he could make himself free from death and other plagues and miseries of life. If he was independent in his own fate, he would never need to be humble facing the world ... Therefore, the inherent need of man to God and a resourceful owner is a part of his existential truth; in other words, poverty and need are destined in his life. It is such a clear fact that everyone admits that in this regard, there is no difference between a wise man and an ignorant one or between a child and an adult.

Therefore, man at every stage of his humanity, clearly understands out that he has an owner and a master; how he not acknowledge this, when he sees him self inherently needy.

Thus, some scholars believe that the verse refers to the fact that man finds himself a needy creature in the worldly life - who needs something beyond his own being- hence, the verse means that God makes human beings aware of their own needs and they confess to His divinity.[1]

It is proved that knowing the nature of man's soul and its characteristics leads to knowledge of Allah (*Ma'rifat Allah*).

The well-known *hadith*, "Whoever knows himself, knows his Lord" refers to this issue.

Worship and Breeding the Soul

إِنَّ الْإِنسَانَ خُلِقَ هَلُوعًا . إِذَا مَسَّهُ الشَّرُّ جَزُوعًا. وَإِذَا مَسَّهُ الْخَيْرُ مَنُوعًا. إِلَّا الْمُصَلِّينَ. الَّذِينَ هُمْ عَلَى صَلَاتِهِمْ دَائِمُونَ. وَالَّذِينَ فِي أَمْوَالِهِمْ حَقٌّ مَّعْلُومٌ.

Indeed man has been created covetous: anxious when an ill befalls him and grudging when good comes his way — [all are such] except the prayerful,

---

1. *Tafsir al-Mizan*. vol.8, p.307, regarding the discussed verse (summarized).

those who are persevering in their prayers and in whose wealth there is a known right. (70: 19-24)

Summary of Commentary:

These verses clearly prove that paying attention to the pure nature of Allah, worshiping, and maintaining prayers directly affect the purification of the soul from the moral vices such as impatience and stinginess.

Another verse of the Qur'an refers to the effect of maintaining prayers and fasting on strengthening man's soul and says, "O you who have faith! Take recourse in patience and prayers; indeed, Allah is with the patient." (2: 153)

In some of the Islamic traditions[1], patience is interpreted as fasting which is one of the clear examples of patience; otherwise, patience is a broad concept that includes any endurance against the passion and the temptations of the devil, and any perseverance in the obedience of Allah and against unfortunate events and afflictions.

In a *hadith* by Imām 'Alī, it is narrated that he used to maintain prayers going to conduct an important job. Then he used to recite

---

1. *Majma' al-Bayan fi-Tafsir al- Qur'an.* vol.1, in regard to the verse (2: 45) which is similar to the discussed verse; and *Tafsir al-Burhan*, vol.1, p.166 regarding the verse (2: 153). A *hadith* by Imām Ṣādiq reads in regard to the verse "Take recourse in patience and prayers" that "Patience is fasting", *Biḥār al-Anwār*, vol.93, p.294.

the verse "Take recourse in patience and prayers"[1] which means "prayers empower me."

These significant worships revive the virtues in man's being such as trust in Allah, courage, patience, and endurance; they keep him away from the moral hindrances like cowardice, fear, hesitation, anxiety, and concern facing important events and world life.

Remembrance of Allah and Breeding the Soul

الَّذِينَ آمَنُواْ وَتَطْمَئِنُّ قُلُوبُهُم بِذِكْرِ اللّهِ أَلاَ بِذِكْرِ اللّهِ تَطْمَئِنُّ الْقُلُوبُ.

> Those who have faith, and whose hearts find rest in the remembrance of Allah. Look! The hearts find rest in Allah's remembrance! (13: 28)

Summary of Commentary:

Discussing the effect of the remembrance of God on the rest of the heart, the rest that can save man from slipping and lead him to the moral virtues, the first verse says, "those who have faith and whose hearts find rest in the remembrance of Allah."

Then it adds the same meaning as a general rule and says, "Look! The hearts find rest in Allah's remembrance!"

---

1. *Uṣūl al-Kāfī* cited in *al-Mizan*, vol.1, p.154.

This great rest is due to the fact that concerns sometimes come about because of the dark and vague future; for example, it comes from the likelihood of the decline of blessings, suffering from illnesses, helplessness, disabilities, and so on; and sometimes it is because of the dark past days of life as well as the affection for the worldly life, suspicion and illusion, and fear of death; each can be a factor for man's concern and discomfort.

Seduction, jealousy, greed and the like are also the factors of man's concern.

Remembrance of God, who is the Generous, the Compassionate, the Merciful, the Creator, the Beneficent and the Provider; Who finds it easy to solve all problems. All complicated issues are simple before His will.

Remembrance of God leads to calmness of the hearts and the cultivation of the moral virtues. It is noteworthy that the soul at peace is the soul that is addressed in this verse, "O soul at peace! Return to your Lord, pleased, pleasing! Then enter among My servants! And enter My paradise!" (89: 27-30)

The Quality of Remembrance

وَاذْكُر رَّبَّكَ فِي نَفْسِكَ تَضَرُّعاً وَخِيفَةً وَدُونَ الْجَهْرِ مِنَ الْقَوْلِ بِالْغُدُوِّ وَالآصَالِ وَلاَ تَكُن مِّنَ الْغَافِلِينَ.

And remember your Lord within your heart beseechingly and reverentially, without being loud, morning and evening, and do not be among the heedless. (7: 205)

Summary of Commentary:

The pioneers of the morality introduce some steps for remembrance:

The first step is remembrance which is a term through which man utters the Name of God, His majesty and elegant attributes, as well as His good names without caring about their concepts and contents; like many people who maintain prayers but just utter the words regardless of their meanings.

Such an utterance is not ineffective. Firstly, it is an introduction to the higher stages; and secondly, it is always combined with a single concept and a brief overview as whoever maintains prayers is fully aware of standing before God and praying before Him although he does not understand the implications in detail. However, it is certainly worthless and does not have much effect on the cultivation of his soul and the refinement of his morality.

The second step is the spiritual remembrance; that is, in uttering the verbal remembrance, man should pay attention to its meanings. Paying attention to the meanings and concepts of remembrance, especially the difference between these concepts and their characteristics, deepens the remembrance and has more profound effects on man's cultivation. Man feels the effects of the remembrance by its repetition.

The third step is the wholehearted remembrance which means

to pay attention to the Lord sincerely first and then to utter it verbally. For instance, reviewing the works of God in the world of creation and observing the extraordinary order of the universe and its delicacy remind man of the majesty of God, "Allah is Almighty and Merciful!" This is a sincere remembrance that expresses a state of man's soul.

Sometimes man finds a spiritual presence in his soul, and without an intermediate, he utters the words "O Holy", "O Pure", or the terms like "Glory to you, O Allah, there is no God but You."

These wholehearted terms of remembrance have tremendous effects on self-perfection and the cultivation of the moral virtues.

The Holy Qur'an refers to the steps of remembrance and states, "So celebrate the Name of your Lord and dedicate yourself to Him with total dedication." (73: 8)

In another verse, He says, "And remember your Lord within your heart beseechingly and reverentially, without being loud, morning and evening, and do not be among the heedless." (7: 205)

The first verse pays deep attention to the verbal remembrance and eventually it leads to chastity and devotion of life to God; that is to say, to leave everything and join God.

In the second verse, attention is paid to the wholehearted remembrance that is mixed with supplication and fear of God and leads to a hidden verbal remembrance, which originates from the soul and is uttered verbally.

Impediments of Remembrance

يَا أَيُّهَا الَّذِينَ آمَنُوا لَا تُلْهِكُمْ أَمْوَالُكُمْ وَلَا أَوْلَادُكُمْ عَن ذِكْرِ اللَّهِ وَمَن يَفْعَلْ ذَلِكَ فَأُولَئِكَ هُمُ الْخَاسِرُونَ.

O you who have faith! Do not let your possessions and children distract you from the remembrance of Allah, and whoever does that—it is they who are the losers. (63: 9)

Summary of Commentary:

Verbal remembrance does not pose significant obstacles because whenever man wishes, he can utter the sacred remembrances (*zikr* pl. *azkār*) containing the Holy names of God and His elegant and perfect attributes, unless he is so busy or distracted from the world that he is not even able to mention such words of remembrance. However, the wholehearted and spiritual remembrance encounters many impediments while the most important of them is man himself, although God is omnipresent and nearer to us than ourselves, "and We are nearer to him than his jugular vein." (50: 16)

He is before and after everything, and He is with everything. According to a famous Alawi tradition, "I did not see anything except God before it, after it, and with it! ("Before it" because

He is the Creator, "after it" because everything is mortal and He remains, and "with it" because He is the Keeper and the Caretaker of everything!)." However, it is very likely that the evil traits and actions of man are such a thick veil over his eyes that he never feels his presence before God; as the famous prayer of Imām Sajjād ﷺ (Dua *Abū Hamzah al-Thumālī*) reads, "You are never hidden from Your creatures unless their deeds become a veil before You!" And the most important of these veils is "selfishness" that prevents man from "knowledge of Allah" and "remembrance of Allah".

The selfish man cannot know God; selfishness is a kind of polytheism that is not compatible with the truth of monotheism.

A *hadith* by Imām 'Alī ﷺ reads, "Anything that neglects man from the remembrance of God is from Satan!"[1]

And in another *hadith* from Imām 'Alī ﷺ, he is narrated to have said, "Anything that makes man neglect God is a kind of gambling!" [2] (According to the Holy Qur'an, gambling is a kind of idolatry)[3].

God says, "O you who have faith! Do not let your possessions and children distract you from the remembrance of Allah, and whoever does that—it is they who are the losers." [4]

Following this verse, a *hadith* is quoted from the Prophet ﷺ

---

1. *Mizan al-Hikmah*. vol.2, p.975, (New edition, discussion on remembrance).
2. Ibid.
3. (5: 90).
4. (63: 9).

saying, "The believers are the good servants of my nation who by no means neglect the remembrance of Allah and the five daily prayers."[1]

Role Models and Exemplars

لَقَدْ كَانَ لَكُمْ فِي رَسُولِ اللَّهِ أُسْوَةٌ حَسَنَةٌ لِّمَن كَانَ يَرْجُو اللَّهَ وَالْيَوْمَ الْآخِرَ وَذَكَرَ اللَّهَ كَثِيرًا.

In the Apostle of Allah there is certainly for you a good exemplar, for those who look forward to Allah and the Last Day and remember Allah greatly. (33: 21)

Summary of Commentary

Everyone tries to follow a model and internalize their traits within their own life. In other words, man is obsessed in leaders and heroes; and for this reason, people of the world follow the real historical heroes and oftentimes fantasy figures. They base a part of their culture and history on the heroes' existence, they talk about them in their meetings and admire them; they try to follow them in terms of traits and morality.

Additionally, the principle of emulating others, especially famous figures, is one of the definitive psychological principles.

---

1. *Mizan al-Hikmah*. vol.2, p.975, (New edition).

According to this principle, man has a tendency to coordinate and emulate with others (especially with perceived heroes); therefore, he is interested in their deeds and characteristics.

This interest is much stronger when man believes in the given figure deeply. For this reason, there are two principles in Islam named "Loving God's servants" (*Tawallā*) and "Disliking God's enemies" (*Tabarrā*); both are a manifestation of this psychological phenomenon. According to these two principles, man is obliged to like God's friends and dislike God's enemies, and follow the great leaders of Islam, the Prophet ﷺ and the infallible Imāms in all affairs.

In the aforementioned verse, God refers to The Holy Prophet ﷺ, addressing his companions saying: "In the Apostle of Allah there is certainly for you a good exemplar, for those who look forward to Allah and the Last Day and remember Allah greatly." Whoever disobeys (the examplar of these men of God) (and makes a plan of friendship with the enemies of God, he hurts himself and God does not need him). Whereas one who emulates is self-contained and deserves to be praised by everybody.

This verse focuses on the fact that "Loving God's servants" and "Disliking God's servants" are the outcomes of faith in God and Resurrection; moreover, God is not in need of this loving or disliking. Man needs to follow these principles for his own spiritual evolution and peace in his society.

The verse deals with the Battle of Aḥzāb (the Battle of the Tribes) where the Prophet ﷺ resisted strongly, arranged the

PRACTICAL STEPS TOWARDS MORAL PURIFICATION

warriors correctly, chose the best military methods, and broke the unity of the enemy. Together with the believers, he took the dagger and dug the trench, and joked with his companions to keep them ready. He did not ignore God's remembrance for a moment and promised his followers the brilliant future and great conquests.

Thus, the small group of Muslims dominated the huge group of the enemy parties. This resistance was an example for all.

Therefore, the Qur'an says, "In the Apostle of Allah there is certainly for you a good exemplar, for those who look forward to Allah and the Last Day and remember Allah greatly."

The Prophet ﷺ was a model not only in the Battle of Aḥzāb, which was an example of *al-jihad al-Asghar*, but also in the struggle against the misdeeds and in the moral refinement, *al-jihad al-Akbar*.

Morality: A Quranic Perspective

Part Two
Details of Moral Problems

Pride and Arrogance

$$\text{وَإِذْ قُلْنَا لِلْمَلائِكَةِ اسْجُدُوا لآدَمَ فَسَجَدُوا إِلا إِبْلِيسَ أَبَى وَاسْتَكْبَرَ وَكَانَ مِنَ الْكَافِرِينَ.}$$

And when We said to the angels, 'Prostrate before Adam,' they prostrated, but not Iblis: he refused and acted arrogantly, and he was one of the faithless. (2: 34)

Summary of Commentary:

The verses of the Holy Qur'an are full of the stories of arrogance and the miseries and problems occurred in societies because of this abhorrent trait.

This verse discusses Iblīs and his famous story, when God ordered all the angels to prostrate for the creation of mankind - at that time Iblīs was one of the ranks of the angels because of his magnificence position- all prostrated except Iblīs, who disobeyed this command of God and arrogantly became a faithless.

Due to this obvious disobedience together with the protest the nature of the command, God says, "'Get down from it!' He said. 'It is not for you to be arrogant therein. Begone! You are indeed among the degraded ones.'" (7: 13)

In fact, this is the first sin that occurred in the world, a sin that reduced years of worship due to his arrogance in a very short time. One who had worshiped God for many years and according to Imām 'Alī ﷺ - in the *khutbah al- Qāsi'ah*- for six thousand years.

In this deterrent story, there are so many important points about the dangers of arrogance, and it is well inferred that this vile trait may eventually lead to disbelief and infidelity, as was stated in the verses above.

This story also indicates that Iblīs was oblivious of the most obvious issues because of the dangerous veil of pride and arrogance. When he came to protest against God, he said: 'I will not prostrate before a human whom You have created out of a dry clay [drawn] from an aging mud'. (15: 33)

Clearly, the dignity of Adam was not due to be brought into existence of mud, but because of the same divine spirit that the Qur'an refers to in the previous verses.

Additionally, there are many people who make a mistake; but finding it out, they repent and reform. However, for some, arrogance and pride even do not allow them to return after they discover their mistake! Thus, Satan did not repent when he realized his mistake because his arrogance did not allow him to prostrate before the great phenomenon of the creation (mankind), but he went on his obstinacy and swore to mislead all human beings, except for God's real faithful. He was not satisfied with this and asked God the eternal life to go on his job to the end of the world!

Thus, selfishness and arrogance are the results of obstinacy, infidelity, jealousy, disobeying the truth, destruction, and corruption of the creation of God.

Humility and Modesty

وَعِبَادُ الرَّحْمَنِ الَّذِينَ يَمْشُونَ عَلَى الْأَرْضِ هَوْنًا وَإِذَا خَاطَبَهُمُ الْجَاهِلُونَ قَالُوا سَلَامًا.

The servants of the All-beneficent are those who walk humbly on the earth, and when the ignorant address them, say, 'Peace!' (25: 63)

Summary of Commentary:

In this verse, the reference is made to one of the most outstanding attributes and moral virtues of a group of God's special servants. Verses 63-74 in Sura al-Furqān lists twelve great virtues of this group of the faithful, and the first one is humility. This confirms that as arrogance is the most dangerous vice, humility is the most important or one of the most important virtues. God says, "The servants of the All-beneficent are those who walk humbly on the earth." He adds then, "and when the ignorant address them, say, 'Peace!'"

This verse discusses the humility of this group of servants towards the pure nature of Allah ﷻ. God says, "Those who spend the night for their Lord, prostrating and standing [in worship]" (25: 64).

In his book entitled "*Mufradāt*", Rāghib writes that the word "humble" has two meanings. One of them is the humiliation that is in the nature of mankind and is worthy of praise (then he refers to the verse in question) and a hadith from the Prophet ﷺ who is narrated to have said "the believer is humble."[1]

The second virtue is the humiliation imposed upon man by another person and makes him despicable.

The sentence "those who walk humbly on the earth" does not mean that they only walk humbly, but it also means to deny any selfishness and arrogance that are apparent in all deeds of mankind and even in the quality of his walking as the easiest act. Moral traits always manifest themselves in the context of man's speech and behaviors to the extent that many of his moral traits can be seen in the many ways he walks.

The first indication of God's special servants is their humility that influences all parts of their existence and is even manifested in their walking. And when in verse 37 of Sura al-Isrā, God orders to the Prophet, "Do not walk exultantly on the earth", it is not just about walking, but the humility in all affairs as a sign of being God's servant and worship Him.

---

1. *Kanz al-ʿUmmâl*. No of *hadith*, 290.

Greed and Low Temper

إِنَّ الْإِنسَانَ خُلِقَ هَلُوعًا. إِذَا مَسَّهُ الشَّرُّ جَزُوعًا. وَإِذَا مَسَّهُ الْخَيْرُ مَنُوعًا.

Indeed man has been created covetous: anxious when an ill befalls him and grudging when good comes his way (70: 19-21).

Summary of Commentary:

In regard to the meaning of the word covetous, it seems that the term refers to three negative moral aspects that are greed, impatience, and stinginess. In fact, the commentary following the word "covetous" in the two aforementioned verses makes the real meaning of this word clear and includes all the three implications.

The verses above blame the greedy, mean and stingy people. "Greed" is the source of "stinginess" because the greedy man would like to keep everything for himself. Greed also leads sometimes to anxiety because whenever the greedy man loses some of his facilities, he is distracted and impatient.

The verses above confirm that man is created with these traits, but the question is why he is created so, while we know that the Wise God creates man for felicity and He does not make such defects as the greatest obstacle to his happiness.

To answer this question, some argue that these traits are related to the unfaithful individuals. A faithful man is provided with patience and generosity; but when he is unfaithful, he is naturally anxious facing with the least disadvantages because he has no support to rely on to solve the problems, and he also becomes greedy as he is hopeless of God's grace, Who is the owner of the unseen world treasures and the source of all blessings. The evidence of this commentary is the next verses which exclude the faithful who maintain the prayers.

The Love of the World

اعْلَمُوا أَنَّمَا الْحَيَاةُ الدُّنْيَا لَعِبٌ وَلَهْوٌ وَزِينَةٌ وَتَفَاخُرٌ بَيْنَكُمْ وَتَكَاثُرٌ فِي الْأَمْوَالِ وَالْأَوْلَادِ كَمَثَلِ غَيْثٍ أَعْجَبَ الْكُفَّارَ نَبَاتُهُ ثُمَّ يَهِيجُ فَتَرَاهُ مُصْفَرًّا ثُمَّ يَكُونُ حُطَامًا وَفِي الْآخِرَةِ عَذَابٌ شَدِيدٌ وَمَغْفِرَةٌ مِنَ اللَّهِ وَرِضْوَانٌ وَمَا الْحَيَاةُ الدُّنْيَا إِلَّا مَتَاعُ الْغُرُورِ.

Know that the life of this world is just play and diversion, and glitter, and mutual vainglory among you and covetousness for wealth and children—like the rain whose vegetation impresses the farmer; then it withers and you see it turn yellow, then it becomes chaff, while in the Hereafter there is a severe punishment and forgiveness from Allah and His pleasure; and the life of this world is nothing but the wares of delusion. (57: 20)

Summary of Commentary:

In many cases, the Qur'an considers the life of the world as a kind of childish play and entertainment.

In the verse above, God likens the worldly-minded individuals to children who are unaware of everything and only entertainment and play, they even do not feel the dangers in their surroundings.

Some commentators divide human life into five periods (from childhood to forty), and they consider eight years for each period. In their view, the first eight years are passed playing, the next eight years for fun and entertainment, the next eight years at the young age for beauty and appearance, the next eight years for boasting and self-praising, and finally, in the last eight years, man seeks wealth and power while his personality is stabilized, and this state may go on until the end of his life and thus leave no means for him to think about the spiritual life and the eternal values.

In other verses, the Qur'an considers the world life as the factor of "deception and delusion" and reads, "The life of this world is nothing but the wares of delusion." (3: 185)

Another verse of the Qur'an reads, "So do not let the life of the world deceive you, nor let the Deceiver deceive you concerning Allah." (31: 33)

These verses confirm that the deceptive world is one of the major obstacles in man's spiritual evolution. Greed in the worldly life is like a mirage that attracts a thirsty man in the burning wilderness, but when he runs towards, he finds nothing to quench his thirst; instead, running in this burning wilderness makes him thirstier. Then, he sees the mirage farther; he runs towards it again, but he cannot find anything while he is still thirsty and thirstier until he perishes.

There are many people who have followed the world life for many years; when they get it, they declare that not only they have not found their lost (peace and comfort), but also they found out the happiness of life together with its gloom; the same as "nectar" together with "poison" or "a flower" with "its thorn". Instead of keeping rest and peace, they increase their worries and anxieties to preserve what they have.

Envy

وَمِن شَرِّ حَاسِدٍ إِذَا حَسَدَ.

And from the evil of the envious one when he envies.
(113: 5)

Summary of Commentary:

The fifth verse of Sura al-Falaq refers to the evil of the envious ones and orders the Prophet ﷺ to seek God's protection from their evils. At the beginning of this Sura, the verses ask the Prophet ﷺ to say, 'I seek the protection of the Lord of the daybreak from the evil of what He has created.'

They then point to the three groups of the evil creatures that are the basis of evil and the main cause of wickedness in the world:

The first group is the evil invaders who use the darkness of the night and attack humans while sleeping or awake ("and from the evil of the dark night when it settles"). Here, the term "the dark night" is interpreted as (the evil one that attacks at night) because not only the wild animals come out of their lair and hunt at night, but also the evil and impure ones often use the night-darkness to reach their goals.

However, "darkness" here has a wide meaning including any ignorance and secrecy because bandits always use ignorance of people and attack the faithful ones with their ominous and secret plans.

Then the Sura refers to the evils who blow on the knots, and this interpretation refers to the tempting women who are like witches and read spells and blow on the knots; they repeat these baseless enchantments to people's ears and use these temptations to loosen their will in order to pave the way for the attack of the devil's army, "and from the evil of the witches who blow on knots."

Then the Sura points to the third and last group of the evils, saying, "And from the evil of the envious one when he envies."

It is concluded that one of the major causes of destruction and corruption in the world is those destructions and corruptions that originate from envy; thus, the three important sources of evil and corruption (the evil of dark night who use darkness and attack the people, the evil of the witches who use temptations to weaken people's beliefs and loosen their ties with each other, and the evil of the envious who always destroy) are expressed in shortly as a sign of the harmful effects of envy.

The description at the beginning of the verse in regard to God (the Lord of the daybreak) indicates that the triple evil groups always use ignorance, disagreement, and disbelief of people; that if this darkness turns into the brightness of science, unity and faith, their tricks will be useless.

Pride and Selfishness

وَنَادَىٰ فِرْعَوْنُ فِي قَوْمِهِ قَالَ يَا قَوْمِ أَلَيْسَ لِي مُلْكُ مِصْرَ وَهَذِهِ الْأَنْهَارُ تَجْرِي مِن تَحْتِي أَفَلَا تُبْصِرُونَ. أَمْ أَنَا خَيْرٌ مِّنْ هَذَا الَّذِي هُوَ مَهِينٌ وَلَا يَكَادُ يُبِينُ.

And Pharaoh proclaimed amongst his people. He said, 'O my people! Does not the kingdom of Egypt belong to me and these rivers that run at my feet? Do you not perceive? Am I not better than this humble one who cannot even speak clearly? (43: 51-52)

Summary of Commentary:

Referring to the story of Pharaoh, these verses discuss the unpleasant aspects of the wicked trait i.e., pride and selfishness. The verses reveal that pride and arrogance had filled pharaoh's mind so much that he not only ignored the clear reasons of Moses ﷺ but also justified his disobedience with his childish words.

Then the Pharaoh resorted to a clumsy saying that if Moses was right, "Why have no bracelets of gold been cast upon him, nor have the angels come with him as escorts?" (43: 53)

Like Pharaohs and Nimrods, proud people are not careful of their speech due to their ignorance and pride; many times they utter foolish words that even their loved ones laughed at in their hearts. This certainly prevents the penetration of divine knowledge and knowing lifes realities.

Moses ﷺ used to suffer from stuttering during his childhood and when he became a prophet and asked God to solve his speaking problem, God realized his request; however, the Pharaoh ignored the new situation and referred to his former stuttering state.

Long-term Ambitions

ذَرْهُمْ يَأْكُلُواْ وَيَتَمَتَّعُواْ وَيُلْهِهِمُ الْأَمَلُ فَسَوْفَ يَعْلَمُونَ.

Leave them to eat and enjoy and to be diverted by longings. Soon they will know. (15: 3)

Summary of Commentary:

In this verse and addressing the Prophet of Islam ﷺ, Allah ﷻ refers to the infidels and polytheists and says, "Leave them to eat and enjoy and to be diverted by longings. Soon they will know."

They are like livestock that does not understand anything except for water and grass. The only difference they have with these animals and make them lower than the animals is a bunch of long-term ambitions filling their minds so full that they are unable to think about their destiny, avoid ignorance and go back to the right path before they pass away.

Here, the negative influence of long [worldly] ambitions in

man's existence is well explained and shows how much the wishes engage man and make him neglect God.

The phrase "leave them" clearly indicates that there was no hope to guide this group; otherwise, the Prophet ﷺ would have never been ordered to leave them.

How one can be hopeful to lead a group whose ultimate goal is to eat and sleep like animals, and long-term [worldly] ambitions do not allow them to think for a moment about the end of life, about the Creator who provides them with these life benefits, and about the purpose for which are created.

Islamic narrations with various interpretations condemn long-term wishes; for instance, Imām 'Alī ؏ says, "The previous nations were tormented just because of their long ambitions and forgetting the end of their life until the time of the promised doom, the doom when any apologize will be rejected and the doors of repentance will be closed."[1]

Fear God

الَّذِينَ يُبَلِّغُونَ رِسَالَاتِ اللَّهِ وَيَخْشَوْنَهُ وَلَا يَخْشَوْنَ أَحَدًا إِلَّا اللَّهَ وَكَفَى بِاللَّهِ حَسِيبًا.

Such as deliver the messages of Allah and fear Him, and fear no one except Allah, and Allah suffices as reckoner. (33: 39)

---

1. *Nahj al-balāgha,* No of *khutbah,* 147.

Morality: A Quranic Perspective

Summary of Commentary:

One of the moral vices is the improper fear that causes man's degradation, contempt, and retardation; the fear that destroys man's wishes and allows the enemy to dominate him.

The opposite of fear is the courage that is the main cause of victory and the most basic foundation of man's pride and majesty. For this reason, the scholars of morality discuss "fear" and "courage" extensively, and analyze their relevant factors, outcomes, effects, and consequences.

In the verse discussed, one of the special traits of the prophets ﷺ with the divine missions was not to fear of anything else except for God. The realization of the divine mission is the most important duty of the Prophets of God ﷺ, and its main requirement is to avoid fear.

Referring to the previous Prophets ﷺ, this verse warns, first of all the Prophet of Islam ﷺ and then all his true followers, not to fear anything except God in performing the divine mission. It means the hideous people are not worthy of this mission and not able to do this!

Some commentators believe that this verse was revealed due to the fact that in their missions, the divine Prophets ﷺ should not do dissimulation (*Taqiya*). This is true when dissimulation means to fear the opponents; but dissimulation is not always due to fear, sometimes it intends to attract the opponents gradually and lead them to the divine goals, and perhaps the Prophet Ibrāhīm's ﷺ words, "this is my Lord", against those who were worshiping stars, the Moon, and the Sun, refer to this point.

Trust

وَيَرْزُقْهُ مِنْ حَيْثُ لَا يَحْتَسِبُ وَمَن يَتَوَكَّلْ عَلَى اللَّهِ فَهُوَ حَسْبُهُ إِنَّ اللَّهَ بَالِغُ أَمْرِهِ قَدْ جَعَلَ اللَّهُ لِكُلِّ شَيْءٍ قَدْرًا.

And provide for him from whence he does not reckon. And whoever puts his trust in Allah, He will suffice him. Indeed Allah carries through His command. Certainly Allah has set a measure for everything. (65: 3)

Summary of Commentary:

Many verses of the Holy Qur'an, Islamic narrations, the Prophets' life stories and the books authored by the scholars of morality and mystical wayfaring (*Seyr-u Suluk*) are concerned with trust as an important moral virtue without which one cannot be in proximity to God (*Qurb-e-Elahi*). Trust means to entrust all the affairs to the Lord and believe in His favor.

Pointing out the clear outcome of entrusting to Allah, this verse encourages all individuals to put their trust in Allah, and promises their salvation and triumph. In fact, God gives a definite promise to solve the problems of all those who place their trust in Him. Then He refers to the reason and says, "Certainly Allah has set a measure for everything."

Obviously, Allah is able to fulfill all His promises and solve the problems, no matter how difficult and complicated they are, by His will and commands. The sentence "Certainly, Allah has set a measure for everything" answers the question why sometimes we have the ultimate confidence in His pure nature, but the victories are delayed.

The Qur'an responds to this question that we are not aware of the matter of the affairs. Everything has its own reason, every task requires its own proper time, and every phenomenon is desirable in its own particular context; therefore, based on what Imām 'Alī ﷺ said, the occurrence of the affairs depend on their own time, sometimes the results should be delayed; thus, in such matters one should not hurry.

Similar to this meaning, verse 160 of Sura *Āle 'Imrān* finds the origin of victory and failure from God and says that putting their trust in God, the faithful are winners, "If Allah helps you, no one can overcome you, but if He forsakes you, who will help you after Him? So in Allah let all the faithful put their trust."

In Islamic narratives, the great importance is given to this moral value, including in the *hadith* of Imām 'Alī ﷺ, who said, "One who trusts in God, problems will be easy for him to solve."[1]

Appetites Desire

وَاللّٰهُ يُرِيدُ أَن يَتُوبَ عَلَيْكُمْ وَيُرِيدُ الَّذِينَ يَتَّبِعُونَ الشَّهَوَاتِ أَن تَمِيلُوا مَيْلًا عَظِيمًا.

Allah desires to turn toward you clemently, but those

---

1. *Ghurar Al-Hikam*. No. 9028.

who pursue their [base] appetites desire that you fall into gross waywardness. (4: 27)

Summary of Commentary:

The phrase "appetites desire" in lexicon has a general concept that refers to any desire of self and desire for material pleasures. Appetite desire refers in addition to the general concept of sexual desire.

Making a clear distinction between "repenting" and "pursuing appetite desire" and pointing out that these two issues move in two opposite directions, the verse reads, "Allah desires to turn toward you clemently, but those who pursue their [base] appetites desire that you fall into gross waywardness."

Those who are full of sins and lust would like to lead others to sins; while God wants people to avoid sins, to repent and return to Him, and to follow in knowledge and light, the virtues of piety, felicity and fortune.

According to great commentators, the meaning of "gross waywardness" is to violate the divine rules and commit different kinds of sins. Some also interpret this term as to have illegal sexual relationships with the family members that is forbidden in the previous verses - which in fact is one of the implications of the aforementioned concept.

It should be noted that "pursue their [base] appetites desire" in this verse may have the same general meaning; it may also refer to "sexual lust" because this verse follows the verses that discuss illegal sexual relationships with family members, the married women, and maidens (due to lack of chastity). However, this verse is a clear proof that the path of "lust" is separated from "theology" and that these two are opposite.

Appetites desire is received a considerable attention in Islamic narrative resources which mostly warn about its dangerous consequences.

For instance, Imām 'Alī ﷺ says, the lust is a killing poison (that destroys man's personality, faith, compassion, and value).[1]

Chastity and Fervor

قَالَتْ فَذَلِكُنَّ الَّذِي لُمْتُنَّنِي فِيهِ وَلَقَدْ رَاوَدْتُهُ عَن نَّفْسِهِ فَاسْتَعْصَمَ وَلَئِن لَّمْ يَفْعَلْ مَا آمُرُهُ لَيُسْجَنَنَّ وَلَيَكُوناً مِّنَ الصَّاغِرِينَ. قَالَ رَبِّ السِّجْنُ أَحَبُّ إِلَيَّ مِمَّا يَدْعُونَنِي إِلَيْهِ وَإِلاَّ تَصْرِفْ عَنِّي كَيْدَهُنَّ أَصْبُ إِلَيْهِنَّ وَأَكُن مِّنَ الْجَاهِلِينَ.

She said, 'He is the one on whose account you blamed me. Certainly I did solicit him, but he was continent, and if he does not do what I bid him, surely he shall be imprisoned and be among the abased.' He said, 'My Lord! The prison is dearer to me than to what they invite me. If You do not turn away their schemes from me, then I will incline towards them and become one of the senseless.' (12: 32-33)

---

1. *Ghurar Al-Hikam*. No of *hadith*, 876.

Summary of Commentary:

"Chastity" is the opposite of gluttony and lust; it means a state of soul that prevents man from lust.

"Fervor" is also one of the terms discussed in Islamic teachings as an important moral virtue; in religion, it means defend the family, property, or country strongly.

This verse describes the life of Yūsuf ﷺ and his righteousness, it also points out the divine test happened like a severe storm before him, "When she heard of their machinations, she sent for them and arranged a repast, and gave each of them a knife, and said [to Joseph], 'Come out before them.' So when they saw him, they marveled at him and cut their hands [absent-mindedly]." (12: 31)

She said, "He is the one on whose account you blamed me. Certainly I did solicit him, but he was continent, and if he does not do what I bid him, surely he shall be imprisoned and be among the abased." (12: 32)

This was a difficult test for Yūsuf ﷺ. He faced a dilemma; to accept the request of the chieftain's wife and enjoy her kindness, blessing, and affection or to reject her request, being imprisoned and bear the difficult situation.

He chose his own way without a doubt and turned to God Almighty and said, "My Lord! The prison is dearer to me than to what they invite me. If You do not turn away their schemes from me, then I will incline towards them and become one of the senseless." (12: 33)

This interpretation refers to Yūsuf's chastity and infallibility, as well as his fervor and piety. It is clear from the interpretation of the verse that the women of that palace also supported the chieftain's wife and invited Yūsuf to accept her request, and each of them kindly tried to persuade him to respond to her invitation.

In regard to the request of the chieftain's wife and her threat to imprison him, Yūsuf ﷺ said, "My Lord! The prison is dearer to me than to what they invite me. If You do not turn away their schemes from me, then I will incline towards them and become one of the senseless."

The threat was serious and put into practice. Yūsuf ﷺ was imprisoned, but his noble soul was saved from the disgraceful environment of the chieftain's palace. In the next verses, it is stated that God made this terrible prison a platform for the progress of Yūsuf ﷺ.

Negligence

وَمَن يَعْشُ عَن ذِكْرِ الرَّحْمَٰنِ نُقَيِّضْ لَهُ شَيْطَانًا فَهُوَ لَهُ قَرِينٌ.

Whoever turns a blind eye to the remembrance of the All-beneficent, We assign him a devil who remains his companion. (43: 36)

Summary of Commentary:

"Negligence" is a broad and wide-ranging concept that includes to be unaware of the conditions of time and place (in which man lives), of the realities of his past and present and future, of his attributes and actions, of the divine messages and verses, as well as of the warnings given to man by the bad and good events. One of the obvious examples of negligence is to forget the remembrance of God.

In the verse in question and as a general rule - which is true for all ethnic groups and individuals - God says, "Whoever turns a blind eye to the remembrance of the All-beneficent, We assign him a devil who remains his companion."

As it is said in the Holy Qur'an, "Indeed those who say, 'Our Lord is Allah!' and then remain steadfast, the angels descend upon them, [saying,] 'Do not fear, nor be grieved! Receive the good news of the paradise which you have been promised." (41: 30), remembrance of God causes the companionship of man and the angels; whereas "negligence" and "ignorance" of the remembrance of God lead to the friendship of the devils. The devils that dominate over man and take him wherever they want. When He says, "We assign him a devil who remains his companion", He means that man's "negligence" and "ignorance" that lead him to forget God, have such a consequence; in other words, it is the punishment that is imposed on man in the world.

The Prophet ﷺ says in a *hadith* that when God wishes an evil for a servant who ignores God, He sends him an evil one year before his death (which changes everything in his eyes). Then he does not see any good thing unless it seems ugly in his opinion so that he leaves it; and he does not see any bad thing unless it looks marvelous in his opinion and makes him do it."[1]

The discussion of this verse should be concluded with a proper

---

1. *Tafsir Rūḥ al-Bayān*. vol.8, p.369.

piece narrated in *Tafsir Rūḥ al-Bayān:*

   Alas, the evil soul is our companion,
   And the deal brings us the demon's friendship,
   We were in the heaven with the envy of the angles,
   We are here now together with this evil soul

Stinginess

هَاأَنتُمْ هَٰؤُلَاءِ تُدْعَوْنَ لِتُنفِقُوا فِي سَبِيلِ اللَّهِ فَمِنكُم مَّن يَبْخَلُ وَمَن يَبْخَلْ فَإِنَّمَا يَبْخَلُ عَن نَّفْسِهِ وَاللَّهُ الْغَنِيُّ وَأَنتُمُ الْفُقَرَاءُ وَإِن تَتَوَلَّوْا يَسْتَبْدِلْ قَوْمًا غَيْرَكُمْ ثُمَّ لَا يَكُونُوا أَمْثَالَكُمْ.

Ah! There you are, being invited to spend in the way of Allah; yet among you there are those who are stingy; and whoever is stingy is stingy only to himself. Allah is the All-sufficient, and you are all-needy, and if you turn away He will replace you with another people, and they will not be like you. (47: 38)

Summary of Commentary:

The blessings that God provides man with are more than his needs in many cases so that he can share them with others, but a group of people refuse to do so because of the wicked trait of stinginess, they do not share the blessings of God with others.

In the verse in question, God addresses the companions of the Prophet ﷺ and condemns the stingy individuals and says, "Ah! There you are, being invited to spend in the way of Allah; yet among you, there are those who are stingy; and whoever is stingy is stingy only to himself." To prevent the unbelievers to think that God needs these charity, He says, "Allah is the All-sufficient, and you are all-needy."

So whatever man spends for charity is, in fact, the divine gift given to him for his trying and training for a few days, and God commands man to give part of this grant to His poor servants or pay it out for a *jihad*.

At the end of the verse, God threatens the stingy people, "And if you turn away He will replace you with another people, and they will not be like you." In this way, the stingy individuals are threatened with replacement and this is the most severe threat to them.

Although according to the proofs included in the verses, the meaning of charity and spending in the way of God is the charity and spending in the way of *jihad*, its broad concept includes all good deeds.

Many *Shiite* and *Sunni* commentators narrate in regard to the verse that after the revelation of the above verse, a group of the Prophet's companions asked him, "Who are the stingy groups God refers to in the Qur'an whom He will replace with other people and they will not be like them?"

The Prophet put his hand on Salmān's shoulder - or based on another narration, on his foot - sitting near him and said, "God means this man and his tribe, I swear to God whose hands my life is in! If the faith is in at the farthest point of the sky, a group of Persian men will find it." [1]

---

1. This *hadith* is narrated by Qurtubi in *Al-Jāmi' li Aḥkām Al- Qur'an*, al-Brūsawī in *Tafsir Rūḥ ul-Bayān*, Fakhr Razi in *Tafsir al-Kabir*, Maraghi in his commentary, Tabrisi in *Majma' al-Bayan*, Abū al-Fath in his commentary, Suyūṭī in *al-Durr al-Mansour*, and other commentators in regard to the verse.

Munificence and Generosity

وَيُطْعِمُونَ الطَّعَامَ عَلَىٰ حُبِّهِ مِسْكِينًا وَيَتِيمًا وَأَسِيرًا. إِنَّمَا نُطْعِمُكُمْ لِوَجْهِ اللَّهِ لَا نُرِيدُ مِنكُمْ جَزَاءً وَلَا شُكُورًا.

They give food, for the love of Him, to the needy, the orphan and the prisoner, [saying] 'We feed you only for the sake of Allah. We do not want any reward from you nor any thanks. (76: 8-9)

Summary of Commentary

The two terms, munificence and generosity are the opposite of the word "stinginess", are often used in the same sense, however sometimes it is inferred by some words that munificence is a stage higher than generosity.

Munificence and generosity are two important moral virtues. The extent that stinginess is the sign of man's humiliation, as well as the weakness of his faith and the lack of his personality, it is to the same extent that generosity is the sign of ones faith and supreme personality.

The verse in question discusses of those who are hungry and heavily need their own food but give it to the sick, the orphans, and the prisoners without expecting reward and affection, "They give food, for the love of Him, to the needy, the orphan and the prisoner, [saying] 'We feed you only for the sake of Allah. We do not want any reward from you nor any thanks."

Lots of *Shiite* and *Sunni* traditions confirm that verses 8 and 9 of Sura al-Insān (Sura al-Dahr) were revealed on the virtue of the People of the House (*Ahl al-Bayt*). In his book "*al-Ghadir*", the late 'Āllama Amini listed 34 famous *Sunni* scholars who inserted this *hadith* in their works (with the name of the book and the relevant pages).[1]

Therefore, this well-known *hadith* is frequently mentioned by the *Sunni* scholars, and the *Shiite* scholars agree that the whole of Sura al-Dahr or a significant part of its verses were revealed about the *Ahl al-Bayt* of the Prophet ﷺ (specifically 'Alī, Fāṭimah Zahra, Ḥasan, and Ḥusayn).

The verses of this Sura make it clear that how God praises the generous individuals, glorifies their actions, and provides them with the highest rewards. In one verse, they are referred to as benefactors (*Abrar*) and elsewhere as God's special servants (*'Ibādallah*).

In Islamic narrations, there are a lot of interpretations of munificence and generosity that are somewhat unique in nature. The following narrative is an example. In the *hadith* of Imām Sādiq ﷺ, it is read that a young generous sinful man is more beloved by God than an old stingy praying one. [2]

---

1. *Al-Ghadir*. vol. 3, from p. 107 to the next pages. *Ihqaq al-Haq*. vol. 3, pp. 157-171. This *hadith* book includes the name of the 36 *Sunni* scholars and the references of the *hadith*.
2. *Biḥār al-Anwār*, vol.70, p.307.

Hurry and Haste

وَيَدْعُ الإِنسَانُ بِالشَّرِّ دُعَاءهُ بِالْخَيْرِ وَكَانَ الإِنسَانُ عَجُولاً.

Man prays for ill as [avidly as] he prays for good, and man is overhasty. (17: 11)

Summary of Commentary:

As wicked traits, hurry and haste mean doing things before their necessary premises and preconditions are met. Patience and tolerance are moral virtues and the opposite of these vile traits.

In the aforementioned verse, God discusses one of the bad consequences of hurry and haste that man (due to hurriedness) does the evil deeds, as he requires goodness, and man has always been in a hurry, "Man prays for ill as [avidly as] he prays for good, and man is overhasty."

Here, the word "man", repeated both at the beginning and end of the verse, refers to the first nature of human beings. "Prayer" in this verse means to demand and desire, verbally or practically; thus, man's rush to get more benefits sometimes makes it difficult to examine different aspects of the problem and know his misery or felicity, and he puts himself in dangerous situations.

Prayer is sometimes verbal; that is, man demands from his God many things persistently that not only they are not good for him, but also they lead him to his misery; as Imām Ṣādiq says, "Know the way of your felicity and misery; do not ask God anything that will lead to your misery, while you suppose it as the way of your salvation." This saying refers to the verse "Man prays for ill as [avidly as] he prays for good, and man is overhasty." God Almighty says that man asks for evil, as he requires the goodness because man has always been in hurry. [1]

In fact, man sometimes insists on doing deeds rooted in the following of his soul that ends in misery; but because of Satan's devotion and the temptation of the soul, he supposes them good and causes of his felicity, and he feels uncomfortable when they are not accessed; whereas over time, it may be clear that if his need was met, he would be wretched.

Patience

يَا أَيُّهَا الَّذِينَ آمَنُواْ اسْتَعِينُواْ بِالصَّبْرِ وَالصَّلاَةِ إِنَّ اللهَ مَعَ الصَّابِرِينَ.

O you who have faith! Take recourse in patience and prayer; indeed Allah is with the patient. (2: 153)

Summary of Commentary:

Man's life in the world is fraught with such strange a nd multitudes of problems that if he stands against them and endures patience and resistance, he will be successful; but if he becomes intolerant and surrenders to difficulties, he will never get his goals. By patience, it means to endure various problems and incidents,

---

1. Tafsīr Nūr al-Thaqalayn. vol. 1, p. 141.

the opposite of which is impatience, unrest, loss of resistance, and surrender to problems.

In addition to daily life, the case is true in spiritual life as well. In this verse, advising all the believers to be patient and maintain prayers when problems happen, God says, "O you who have faith! Take recourse in patience and prayer; indeed Allah is with the patient."

This verse has a broad concept and includes all kinds of patience and endurance, whether patience in obedience, in evil-doing, or in disasters. Accomplishing an important task needs assistance and support, whether as a *jihad* or anything else; therefore, in order to accomplish an important task, it is necessary to enjoy patience.

Regarding the interpretation of patience to "fasting", it should be said that fasting is one of the clear examples of patience, not its whole concept. Here the question is about the relationship between patience in the broad sense of the word with prayers.

Some commentators argue that the relationship between patience and prayers is that sometimes man is out of patience. This is when maintaining prayers gives him strength, will and trust in God; thus, the power of patience increases by maintaining prayers. In other words, when man turns to God through prayers, he makes himself bound with His infinite power which increases his resistance significantly against the problems that is turned into an invincible power.

For this reason, a *hadith* is narrated by the Prophet ﷺ and sometimes from Imām 'Alī ؑ, both of them are correct, that faced with a significant problem, he used to maintain prayers, think of a solution after the prayers, and recite this verse, "Take recourse in patience and prayer."[1]

However, this verse is one of the most explicit verses that determine the importance of patience as a victory factor in life.

Ambition

تِلْكَ الدَّارُ الْآخِرَةُ نَجْعَلُهَا لِلَّذِينَ لَا يُرِيدُونَ عُلُوًّا فِي الْأَرْضِ وَلَا فَسَادًا وَالْعَاقِبَةُ لِلْمُتَّقِينَ.

This is the abode of the Hereafter which We shall grant to those who do not desire to domineer in the earth nor to cause corruption, and the outcome will be in favor of the God wary. (28: 83)

Summary of Commentary:

Everybody is interested in something; some people are interested in wealth, others in beauty, some seek perfection, others would like high position, and this last group is called the ambitious one. They would like people to respect them and be better than others, the last words should be their words, and nobody should say a word even if they have no wisdom, intuition, or tact. These people are called ambitious, who would like fame and reputation. This

---

1. *Usūl al-Kāfī*. vol. 1, p.154; *Tafsir Rūḥ al-Bayān*. vol. 1, p. 257.

fact is the source of many individual and social corruptions.

In this verse, revealed regarding Qaroun, God gives a general command, "This is the abode of the Hereafter which We shall grant to those who do not desire to domineer in the earth nor to cause corruption, and the outcome will be in favor of the God-wary." The fate of the arrogant, ambitious men is the same as the fate of Qaroun who lost everything for his ambition and arrogance, God's anger ended his disgraceful life and he was always cursed.

Perhaps by interpreting the term "corruption" to "domineer in the earth", it is inferred that an ambitious person eventually causes corruption in the earth and do not attempt to avoid any crimes to achieve their goals.

A *hadith* of Imām 'Alī reads that when he was walking in the markets as the so-called caliph, he used to help the lost people and the needy. Meeting the salespersons and businessmen, he used to recite and interpret this verse for them, "This is the abode of the Hereafter which We shall grant to those who do not desire to domineer in the earth nor to cause corruption, and the outcome will be in favor of the God wary" in such a way to include not only the rulers but also all power holders (in any form and in any case).

In another *hadith* from Imām Ṣādiq, it is narrated that when he recited the verse, he cried and said, "Based on this verse, all wishes have been gone."[1] Perhaps Imām meant that there is a problem since God considers the Hereafter only for those who do not even think of ambition.

---

1. *Tafsir Ali Ibn Ibrahim*, in regard to the verse.

Of the verse above and similar verses, it is confidently inferred that ambition, especially if it is combined with other wicked traits such as arrogance, pride, prejudice, and stubbornness has unpleasant effects on man's life and can cause not only an individual's but also a society's decadence.

Obstinacy and Making Excuses

قَالَ رَبِّ إِنِّي دَعَوْتُ قَوْمِي لَيْلًا وَنَهَارًا. فَلَمْ يَزِدْهُمْ دُعَائِي إِلَّا فِرَارًا. وَإِنِّي كُلَّمَا دَعَوْتُهُمْ لِتَغْفِرَ لَهُمْ جَعَلُوا أَصَابِعَهُمْ فِي آذَانِهِمْ وَاسْتَغْشَوْا ثِيَابَهُمْ وَأَصَرُّوا وَاسْتَكْبَرُوا اسْتِكْبَارًا.

He said, 'My Lord! Indeed I have summoned my people night and day but my summons only increases their evasion. Indeed whenever I have summoned them, so that You might forgive them, they would put their fingers into their ears and draw their cloaks over their heads, and they were persistent [in their unfaith] and disdainful in [their] arrogance. (71: 5-7)

Summary of Commentary:

Obstinacy and making excuses can be regarded as one of the most important barriers to understanding the truth because they make man unable to be in proximity to God (Qurb-e-Elahi) and become more determined in falsehood. By obstinacy and making excuses, it is not meant that man insists on exploring the truth, but it means that after the disclosure of the truth, he would like to insist on falsehood or wrongdoing.

The above verse discusses the obstinacy of the people of Noah ﷺ against that very sympathetic and compassionate Prophet, who tried to guide them day and night.

Noah ﷺ complained of them to God and said, "'My Lord! Indeed I have summoned my people night and day but my summons only increases their evasion. Indeed whenever I have summoned them so that You might forgive them, they would put their fingers into their ears and draw their cloaks over their heads, and they were persistent [in their unfaith] and disdainful in [their] arrogance."

How stubborn and fanatic a man could be to put his fingers in his ears not to hear the truth, and draw his cloak over his head not to see the faces of the right-seekers, and escape from the right?

There is a restriction for antagonism and escaping from the right, but they followed this way disproportionately, and nothing was the main reason except for stubbornness, fanaticism, and despotism.

Among the divine Prophets ﷺ, nobody invited his people as much as Noah ﷺ did. He summoned the people, insisted on his invitation, and spoke for nine hundred and fifty years. The words "day" and "night" may indicate the holding of private meetings at nights and their public meetings during the days. He continued his enlightening invitation, but nobody believed in except for a small group; and on average, only one person believed every twelve years.

The interpretation of "they would put their fingers into their ears" may be pointed to the severity of their escape from the right path, as if they would like to put all their fingers in their ears not to hear the truth.

The interpretation of "but my summons only increases their evasion" indicates that Noah's invitation had a reverse outcome. Hearing the rightful, arrogant and stubborn people's voice increases their obstinacy, like garbage whose pollution is widespread by the rain.

Thanksgiving

وَإِذْ تَأَذَّنَ رَبُّكُمْ لَئِن شَكَرْتُمْ لَأَزِيدَنَّكُمْ وَلَئِن كَفَرْتُمْ إِنَّ عَذَابِي لَشَدِيدٌ.

And when your Lord proclaimed, If you are grateful, I will surely enhance you [in blessing], but if you are ungrateful, My punishment is indeed severe.' (14: 7)

Summary of Commentary:

"Thanksgiving" is the gratitude of blessing, whether verbally or in practice. The theme of "thanksgiving the grateful" is embodied in man's nature. It is the monotheism and theology path that many scholars rely on in the first ideological debates, namely, "the need to know the donor of the blessings."

The discussed verse is the speech of Moses ﷺ the Prophet to the Israelites, who reminds them of one of the most important divine messages saying, "And when your Lord proclaimed, 'If you are grateful, I will surely enhance you [in blessing], but if you are ungrateful, My punishment is indeed severe.'"

This is what Moses ﷺ said to the Israelites when they had been freed from Pharaoh, they had got independence, greatness, freedom, and blessings, but many of them were ungrateful.

The sentence "I will surely enhance you [in blessing]" associated with many emphases, is a definitive divine promise to those who give thanks, whom He adds to their blessings. However, He does not say to the disbelievers that "I will punish you", instead He says, "My punishment is indeed severe." This difference in the interpretation indicates God's ultimate grace and at the same time a strong warning to those who are ungrateful for the blessings they are provided with. The Israelites wandered for forty years in the desert due to their ungratefulness of the provided blessings.

Regarding "thanksgiving", great scholars of morality argue that thanksgiving means the servants of God should use the blessings in a way they are created for. It is as if this statement is extracted from a *hadith* by Imām Ṣādiq ﷺ that "Thanksgiving is to avoid sins."[1]

Ingratitude

وَضَرَبَ اللّٰهُ مَثَلاً قَرْيَةً كَانَتْ آمِنَةً مُطْمَئِنَّةً يَأْتِيهَا رِزْقُهَا رَغَدًا مِّن كُلِّ

---

1. *Uṣūl al-Kāfī*. vol.2, p.95. No *of hadith*, 10; *Tafsīr Nūr al-Thaqalayn*. vol.2, p. 529.

مَكَانٍ فَكَفَرَتْ بِأَنْعُمِ اللهِ فَأَذَاقَهَا اللهُ لِبَاسَ الْجُوعِ وَالْخَوْفِ بِمَا كَانُوا يَصْنَعُونَ.

Allah draws a parable, a town secure and peaceful. Its provision came abundantly from every place. But it was ungrateful toward Allah's blessings. So Allah made it taste hunger and fear because of what they used to do. (16: 112)

Summary of Commentary:

Ingratitude and ungratefulness mean disregarding the blessings and wasting significant moral vices, whether in individual or social life.

Ingratitude and ungratefulness are significant barriers in the evolution of the man's soul, moving towards God, and its purification. These two wicked traits agonize the soul, weaken the conscience, and destroy the faith.

The verse discusses a group provided with the divine blessings, the blessings of security, peace, health, and the spiritual blessings granted by their Prophet ﷺ, but they were ungrateful; then all those blessings were taken back, and the group was divinely punishment. The verse reads, "Allah draws a parable, a town secure and peaceful. Its provision came abundantly from every place. But it was ungrateful toward Allah's blessings. So Allah made it taste hunger and fear because of what they used to do."

Whether this verse refers to a specific land or a general example is a debate among the commentators. Some of them are of this opinion that the verse is regarding the land of Mecca and the interpretation of the sentence "Its provision came abundantly from every place" reinforces this possibility because it is completely in line with the conditions of Mecca; it is a dry and hot land, with no water and vegetation, but enjoys all kinds of the blessings from all over the world due to the blessing of God's House (*Ka'ba*).

The interpretation of the phrase "A town secure and peaceful" confirms this commentary because the Hijaz environment was often insecure. However, Mecca was safe and secure due to the blessing of God's House (*Ka'ba*).

These material blessings reached their peak when the spiritual blessing of the Prophet's mission ﷺ was added, but people of Mecca were ungrateful for these material and spiritual blessings; thus, they suffered from famine and insecurity. Such is the fate of those who are ungrateful for God's blessings.

However, the verse includes a comprehensive and widespread concept covering all the ungrateful groups of the material and spiritual blessings. The people of Mecca were one of the prominent examples. According to some narrations, they suffered from drought, they had to eat carcasses to overcome their starvation, and severe blows struck them in Islam's battles.

Gentleness and Harshness

فَبِمَا رَحْمَةٍ مِنَ اللهِ لِنتَ لَهُمْ وَلَوْ كُنتَ فَظًّا غَلِيظَ الْقَلْبِ لَانفَضُّواْ مِنْ حَوْلِكَ فَاعْفُ عَنْهُمْ وَاسْتَغْفِرْ لَهُمْ وَشَاوِرْهُمْ فِي الْأَمْرِ فَإِذَا عَزَمْتَ فَتَوَكَّلْ عَلَى اللهِ إِنَّ اللهَ يُحِبُّ الْمُتَوَكِّلِينَ.

It is by Allah's mercy that you are gentle to them; and had you been harsh and hardhearted, surely they would have scattered from around you. So excuse them, and plead for forgiveness for them, and consult them in the affairs, and once you are resolved, put your trust in Allah. Indeed Allah loves those who trust in Him. (3: 159)

Summary of Commentary:

In this verse, "gentleness" is discussed as one of the moral attributes of the Prophet ﷺ and one of the factors of his progress in the Islamic society. Therefore, the Prophet's kindness ﷺ was a divine bounty for himself and the entire nation. Moreover, indeed this kindness, gentleness, and goodness of everyone is a blessing.

This commentary refers to the opposite of gentleness: violence, hardheartedness, and harshness which directly affect man's life as people leave him alone; in other words, gentleness is the reason for the connection of human beings, whereas harshness is a source of their dispersion and hatred.

Regarding this point that both "harsh" and "hardhearted" mean the same and both are used to emphasis or convey two different meanings, the late Tabrisi provides the reader with an interesting and comprehensive interpretation in "*Majma' al-Bayan*", "Some have argued that the combination of these two aspects, although both are the same in terms of meaning, is because "harsh" is usually used for violence in speech whereas "hardhearted" is applied for violence in actions that is due to hardship. Therefore, both terms mean violence, but one is violence in speech, and the other is violence in action.

In any case, God gifted the Prophet ﷺ softness and pleasure, so that he was very gentle against the sinful, harsh and violent people. Thus he could attract the most violent people to Islam.

Then, He offers a series of useful commands through which kindness and pleasure are manifested and take practical aspects. He says, "So excuse them, and plead for forgiveness for them, and consult them in the affairs, and once you are resolved, put your trust in Allah. Indeed Allah loves those who trust in Him." In this way, an extraordinary attractiveness was found because of the prophet's existence ﷺ, attracting the most distant people.

This verse is related to the verses of the Battle of Uhud, where the friends and the enemies put the most severe pressure on the Prophet ﷺ. It is evident that, pardon, forgiveness and affectionate behaviour in such circumstances indicate the Prophet's ﷺ cheerfulness and kindness, and few people can keep cool in such difficult situations.

Trusteeship

إِنَّ اللَّهَ يَأْمُرُكُمْ أَن تُؤَدُّوا الْأَمَانَاتِ إِلَىٰ أَهْلِهَا وَإِذَا حَكَمْتُم بَيْنَ النَّاسِ أَن تَحْكُمُوا بِالْعَدْلِ إِنَّ اللَّهَ نِعِمَّا يَعِظُكُم بِهِ إِنَّ اللَّهَ كَانَ سَمِيعًا بَصِيرًا.

Indeed Allah commands you to deliver the trusts to their [rightful] owners, and, when you judge between people, to judge with fairness. Excellent indeed is what Allah advises you. Indeed Allah is all-hearing, all-seeing. (4: 58)

Summary of Commentary:

Trusteeship is one of the best moral virtues, and its value in Islam and humanity is mentioned with great emphasis in the Qur'an and *hadiths*. The scholars of morality attach great importance to it, whereas betrayal is one of the greatest sins and one of the most damned moral vices.

Two commands are explicitly stated in this verse; a command regarding trust and a command regarding justice. God says, "Indeed Allah commands you to deliver the trusts to their [rightful] owners, and, when you judge between people, to judge with fairness. Excellent indeed is what Allah advises you. Indeed Allah is all-hearing, all-seeing."

Although fair administration and fair judgment amongst people have a very high status, delivering the trust to their [rightful] owners has a priority over these two issues which in turn confirms the extraordinary importance of trust. The order mentioned in the verse may be because trust is a general concept that fair judgment among people is one of its examples. After all, trust, in its general sense, includes all official and social positions as the trusts of God and people are in the hands of the owners of those positions.

The focuses on the verse regarding trusteeship and justice as the good advice of the Lord on the one hand, and warn people that God watches their actions on the other hand. It adds double importance to these two issues, namely observing trust and justice.

Fakhr Razi in his book entitled *Tafsir Kabir* points out three branches of trust: "the trusts of the Lord" such as to do the obligations and duties and to avoid sins as well as to watch for the tongue, the eyes and the ears; "the trusts of the people" such as the mutual deposits, to avoid cheating and backbiting, as well as observing justice by the states, and not encouraging the laypeople for the false prejudices and the like; and "the trusts of man to himself" which means to choose what is right for his life in the world and the Hereafter, and not to be surrendered to lust, violence, and the relevant sins.[1]

What is quoted in the revelation of this verse indicates the widespread concept of trust; it is known that after the conquest of Mecca, the Prophet ﷺ called Uthman bin Talha, the key keeper of the *Ka'ba*, and got the key to throwing out all the idols in there. Then, Abbas, the Prophet's ﷺ uncle, requested to keep the key which was a very prominent position, but the Prophet ﷺ rejected his request; and reciting the above verse, he handed over the key to Uthman bin Talha although he was not yet a Muslim.

Truthfulness

قَالَ اللهُ هَذَا يَوْمُ يَنفَعُ الصَّادِقِينَ صِدْقُهُمْ لَهُمْ جَنَّاتٌ تَجْرِي مِن تَحْتِهَا الأَنْهَارُ خَالِدِينَ فِيهَا أَبَدًا رَّضِيَ اللهُ عَنْهُمْ وَرَضُواْ عَنْهُ ذَلِكَ الْفَوْزُ الْعَظِيمُ.

---

1. *Tafsir Kabir*. Fakhr Razi, vol.10, p. 139, in regard to the verse.

Allah will say, 'This day truthfulness shall benefit the truthful. For them there will be gardens with streams running in them, to remain in them forever. Allah is pleased with them, and they are pleased with Him. That is the great success.' (5:119)

Summary of Commentary:

The interpretations of the Holy Qur'an concerning the importance of truthfulness and honesty are unparalleled and unique, including the interpretation of the above verse. Following an intensive discussion regarding the Christians' aberration from monotheism and God's question from Jesus on the Day of Resurrection and regarding this aberration and his excuse from this charge, God says, "Allah will say 'This day truthfulness shall benefit the truthful."

The verse points out that their truthfulness and honesty in the world will help them on the Day of Resurrection and save them (not because their truthfulness on the Day of Resurrection will save them but because anybody cannot do anything on that Day).

Then, referring to their rewards, He says, "For them there will be gardens with streams running in them, to remain in them forever. Allah is pleased with them and they are pleased with Him. That is a great success."

Heaven with its blessings and eternity on the one hand, and God's satisfaction on the other hand, and the interpretation of "the great success" (the great salvation) indicate the high position the truthful enjoy, and perhaps this is because all good deeds can be summed up in truthfulness and honesty.

Obviously, if God is pleased with somebody, He will bless him with whatever he desires; naturally, when all man's desires are fulfilled, he will be pleased, so God's pleasure will lead to his pleasure, and this mutual pleasure is the greatest extent of pleasure, a grant for the honest and truthful servants.

This interpretation (Allah is pleased with them and they are pleased with Him) is mentioned in four parts of the Holy Qur'an. The analysis of these interpretations reflects the magnitude of its meaning; in one part of the Book, it is about the Muhajirun, the Ansar, and the followers; elsewhere, it is about Hezbollah. In the third case, the Book refers to the best servants, and the verse discusses the truthful and reveals that the truthful are Hezbollah, the best servants, and among the Muhajirun, the Ansar, and the followers.

Lie

إِنَّمَا يَفْتَرِي الْكَذِبَ الَّذِينَ لَا يُؤْمِنُونَ بِآيَاتِ اللهِ وَأُولَٰئِكَ هُمُ الْكَاذِبُونَ.

Only those fabricate lies who do not believe in the signs of Allah, and it is they who are the liars. (16: 105)

Summary of Commentary:

In the teachings of Islam, standing against falsehood and lie is emphasized, in so far as they regard the liars as the divine unbelievers and deniers, they declare lies to be the key of all sins and stipulate that as far as man does not leave a lie in any form and in any case, he cannot be faithful.

This verse was revealed when the enemies of Islam and ignorant polytheists were faced with some verses of the Qur'an where some divine commands were replaced by the others due to the changes in the circumstances. Thus, they got an excuse, condemned the Prophet ﷺ, and said that he had a teacher who taught him these verses (by the teacher, they meant two Christian servants called "Yasar" and "Jabr" or a Christian-Roman man named Balaam). However, the Qur'an was revealed in the auspicious Arabic language, whereas all those men were 'Ajam.

As a response, the Qur'an says the Prophet ﷺ recited the divine revelation that the Holy Spirit (*Rūḥ al-Qudus*) revealed to him from God; and faith, truth, and honesty were evident in all his words, those lie who do not believe in God. A lie will not falsify faith, and true believers' tongues will not utter except for the truth.

The phrase "fabricate lies" in fact focuses on the lie of those who both lie and slander, or according to Tabrisi in *Majmaʿ al-Bayān*, it means "invent lies" that is they make lies (fabricate refers to any offence, including polytheism, lie and slander).

The relationship between lie and defamation is the relationship between the absolute public and private. A lie is a word opposite of reality, but slander and defamation mean to attribute bad traits to someone.

The phrase "fabricate lies" may also refer to the leaders of polytheism (shirk) and disbelief who were lying, lies such as describing the Prophet ﷺ as a poet or a magician and other people were following them.

However, the above verse indicates that lie is not consistent with faith; therefore, in this verse's interpretation, a narration reads that the people asked Muhammad the Prophet ﷺ, "Does a believer commit adultery?" He replied, "It is likely." They asked, "Is it possible he does a robbery?" He said, "It is possible." They asked, "O Messenger of Allah, does a believer lie?" He said, "Never", then he recited the above verse. Of course, it should be noted that faith has a series of steps.[1]

Fulfillment the Covenants

وَلاَ تَقْرَبُواْ مَالَ الْيَتِيمِ إِلاَّ بِالَّتِي هِيَ أَحْسَنُ حَتَّى يَبْلُغَ أَشُدَّهُ وَأَوْفُواْ بِالْعَهْدِ إِنَّ الْعَهْدَ كَانَ مَسْئُولاً.

Do not approach the orphan's property except in the best manner until he comes of age. And fulfill the covenants; indeed, all covenants are accountable. (17: 34)

Summary of Commentary:

---

1. Tabrisi in *Majma' al-Bayān*, Abū al-Futūḥ in *Tafsir Ruh al-Jinan*, and al-Brūsawī in *Tafsir Rūḥ al-Bayān* in regard to the verse.

The most important asset of a society is the trust that individuals have in each other. Anything that strengthens this trust and solidarity is the cause of the prosperity and progress of society. In contrast, any damage to trust is the cause of failure and misery. One of the essential things that develop public and private trust is the fulfillment of a covenant, which is one of the most critical moral virtues; on the contrary, breaking the covenant is one of the worst moral vices. The need to fulfill the covenant is in the nature of human beings.

In the verse above and regarding the need to fulfill the covenant, there is an interesting interpretation, He says: "And fulfill the covenants; indeed all covenants are accountable."

The commentators provide different interpretations for the sentence "indeed all covenants are accountable". One of them is the interpretation mentioned above that man is responsible, and the covenant should be fulfilled; it means people will be counted regarding their covenants.

Another interpretation is that the covenant itself will be counted, as the alive, buried infants will be asked as if they are the living and wise creatures and they will be asked whether their rights were fulfilled or not? This is a kind of virtual meaning for emphasis. However, the first comment seems more appropriate.

It should also be noted that in Sura al- Isrā', verses 22-39 include a part of the most significant Islamic commandments from monotheism to the right of parents, from murdering to adultery and the expropriation of the orphans' properties, and from fulfillment the covenants to the functions of the eyes, ears and heart, which show that fulfillment of the covenants is one of the most basic commandments of Islam.

At the end of these commands, He says, "These are among [precepts] that your Lord has revealed to you of wisdom". (17: 39)

There are essential interpretations in Islamic *hadiths* regarding the fulfillment of the covenants, including a narration of Amir al-Mu'minān ﷺ that reads, "The principle of religion is to deliver the trusts and fulfill the covenants." [1]

Logical Argument and Dispute

إِنَّ الَّذِينَ يُجَادِلُونَ فِي آيَاتِ اللَّهِ بِغَيْرِ سُلْطَانٍ أَتَاهُمْ إِنْ فِي صُدُورِهِمْ إِلَّا كِبْرٌ مَّا هُم بِبَالِغِيهِ فَاسْتَعِذْ بِاللَّهِ إِنَّهُ هُوَ السَّمِيعُ الْبَصِيرُ

Indeed those who dispute the signs of Allah without any authority that may have come to them- there is only vanity in their breasts, which they will never satisfy. So seek the protection of Allah; indeed, He is the All-hearing, the All-seeing. (40: 56)

Summary of Commentary:

The best way to explain the facts is the logical argument free of any bias and obstinacy. When the thoughts are joined together, and talent and ingenuity come together, they make everything clear. However, suppose the discussion atmosphere is full of bias,

---

1. *Ghurur al-Hikam*. No of *hadith*, 1762.

obstinacy, selfishness and in one word of controversy and dispute. In that case, it will be so blurry that sometimes the most obvious truths remain hidden, and as discussions continue, more facts will be unavailable. For this reason, in Islam, disputing is firmly blamed and described as one of the great sins because it is the greatest obstacle to find out the right path and the realities.

In this verse, expressing the meaning of dispute as vain, God refers to one of the sources and main motives of this moral vice and says, "Indeed those who dispute the signs of Allah without any authority that may have come to them- there is only vanity in their breasts, which they will never satisfy."

In these cases, the word "authority" means the proof, the reason, and the argument, including the triple matters mentioned in the preceding verse, both personal knowledge and guidance, as well as the guidance by the knowledgeable leaders, and the guidance by the divine Books. He says that the primary source of controversy and dispute is the arrogance and vanity put in man's nature, and that man would like to achieve a great position by conflicting for vain; he will never get it; instead, he will be degraded.

Since this moral vile is one of the devils dangerous traps, the verse reads, "so seek the protection of Allah; indeed, He is the All-hearing, the All-seeing."

In Islamic narratives, it is strictly forbidden to dispute for vain, especially if there is controversy in religious matters. Amir al-Mu'minīn 'Alī says in a *hadith*, "Conflict in religion leads to the corruption of faith and certainty."[1]

---

1. *Ghurar al – Hikam.* No of *hadith*, 1177.

Reconciliation between People

لاَّ خَيْرَ فِي كَثِيرٍ مِّن نَّجْوَاهُمْ إِلاَّ مَنْ أَمَرَ بِصَدَقَةٍ أَوْ مَعْرُوفٍ أَوْ إِصْلاَحٍ بَيْنَ النَّاسِ وَمَن يَفْعَلْ ذَلِكَ ابْتَغَاءَ مَرْضَاتِ اللهِ فَسَوْفَ نُؤْتِيهِ أَجْرًا عَظِيمًا.

There is no good in much of their secret talks, excepting him who enjoins charity or what is good or reconciliation between people, and whoever does that, seeking Allah's pleasure, soon We shall give him a great reward.

Summary of Commentary:

Social life is always full of disputes and contrasts, and one of the branches of the disputes is the controversies occur among people, widespread sometimes and lead to intense quarrels and even bloody fights.

Man must strive for the reconciliation between people, eliminate misunderstandings, create an atmosphere of optimism amongst those involved in a dispute, and solve the problem.

The verse discusses the secret talks that in many cases annoy others and lead to pessimism and suspicion, and sometimes pave the way for the evil and covert plans, He says, "There is no good in much of their secret talks."

Nevertheless, immediately He adds, "Excepting him who enjoins charity or what is good or reconciliation between people."

Moreover, at the end of the verse, He adds a very encouraging expression to these matters, "and whoever does that, seeking Allah's pleasure, soon We shall give him a great reward."

The exclusion of the reconciliation between people from criticism and secret talks on the one hand; and the reconciliation alongside charity and what is good, and the promise of a tremendous reward, on the other hand, all testify the importance of this issue.

Regarding the difference between charity and what is good, some argue that charity means a benevolent loan known as "*Qarḍ al-Hasana*", and some consider a general concept for what is good that includes all good works (so its relationship to charity is the relationship between the absolute public and private).

In the *hadith* of the Prophet ﷺ, it is also stated that one of the best "charities" which God and the Prophet ﷺ are pleased with is "the reconciliation between people" when they are pessimistic about each other and bring them closer together when they are far from each other and miffed.

Therefore, the reconciliation between people is mentioned both independently and as one of the prominent examples of charity and what is good. In other words, since the reconciliation between people is a perfect charity and right, it is metioned separately.

Excuse the Faults and Anger

الَّذِينَ يُنْفِقُونَ فِي السَّرَّاءِ وَالضَّرَّاءِ وَالْكَاظِمِينَ الْغَيْظَ وَالْعَافِينَ عَنِ النَّاسِ وَاللهُ يُحِبُّ الْمُحْسِنِينَ.

Those who spend in ease and adversity, and suppress their anger, and excuse [the faults of] the people, and Allah loves the virtuous. (3: 134)

Summary of Commentary

Anger and wrath are the two most dangerous statuses of man. If they are not avoided, they aremanifested as madness, insanity, and loss of self-control; and many of the dangerous prejudices and crimes man commits happen in such statuses.

In the verse discussed above, giving the promise of the eternal paradise to the righteous which extends to the heavens and earth, and expressing their qualities, God first of all discusses spending in His way and says, "those who spend in ease and adversity"; then He adds, "and suppress their anger"; and as a result of "excuse [the faults of] the people"; and in general, they are virtuous as "Allah loves the virtuous."

In the next verse, they are promised forgiveness and blessings; if they are found sinful, they should remember Allah and repent, then Allah will accept their pardon. The verse confirms that as they forgive others and overlook their mistakes, God will forgive them and ignore their mistakes.

"Suppressing anger" in this verse is one of the distinguishing features of the righteous and is expressed in the first rank.

Islamic narrations include strange and shocking interpretations about anger and wrath that reveal this moral vice's disadvantage. One of them is a tradition by Imām 'Alī ﷺ, "The strongest enemy of man is the wrath and his soul. Anyone who can restrain these two, he will raise his grade and reach the last stage of perfection."[1]

Conciliation and Revenge

وَجَزَاءُ سَيِّئَةٍ سَيِّئَةٌ مِثْلُهَا فَمَنْ عَفَا وَأَصْلَحَ فَأَجْرُهُ عَلَى اللهِ إِنَّهُ لَا يُحِبُّ الظَّالِمِينَ.

The requital of evil is an evil like it. So whoever excuses and conciliates, his reward lies with Allah. Indeed He does not like the wrongdoers. (42: 40).

Summary of Commentary:

One of the greatest moral virtues that it is not easy to achieve is excuse and conciliation when one is in power and to ignore revenge. Many people keep grudges in their hearts and constantly wait for a day to overcome the enemy and take revenge on him several times. They requite the evil and add wrongdoing to the previous evils, and sometimes they are proud of this vicious trait.

In the verse discussed, God first refers to counteraction and calls

---

1. *Sharh al-Ghurur*. vol.2, p.459, No of *hadith*, 3469.

it the believers' right (so that the enemies and wrongdoers do not find themselves in safety). He then points to conciliation and ignoring revenge and says, "The requital of evil is an evil like it. So whoever excuses and conciliates, his reward lies with Allah. Indeed He does not like the wrongdoers."

Given that Sura al-Shūrā was revealed in Mecca and that at that time the believers were exposed to a wide range of opponents, the Qur'an instructs them not to surrender against oppression in verse 39 of this Sura. When they are oppressed, they should seek help from others and help each other. Then, in verse 40, it refers to the fact that man should not take revenge because some of his friends were oppressed, he should not stoop the wrongdoers' level; he should conciliate even if his deed does not have any harmful effects.

What is meant by conciliation following excuse in this verse? Commentators have various interpretations; some of them refer to the conciliation between themselves and God, some others point to the conciliation between the oppressed and the oppressor to prevent the repetition of the oppression; some others mean conciliation as to avoid revenge, anger, and wrath; and some others point to retribution. [1]

The combination of these meanings in the overall interpretation of this verse is also unlikely. However, the verse demonstrates the fact that excuse and conciliation that follows intorder to eradicate the roots of the grudges forever, and the interpretation of "his

---

1. *Tafsir al-Mizan, Tafsir al-Qurtubi, Tafsir 'Isna 'Ashari, Tafsir Rūḥ al-Bayān,* and *Fi Zilal al- Qur'an* in regard to the verse.

reward lies with Allah" without determining a particular reward even paradise, show that the rewards for such a person are so great that only God is aware of them.

Suspicion, Spying and Backbiting

يَا أَيُّهَا الَّذِينَ آمَنُوا اجْتَنِبُوا كَثِيرًا مِنَ الظَّنِّ إِنَّ بَعْضَ الظَّنِّ إِثْمٌ وَلَا تَجَسَّسُوا وَلَا يَغْتَبْ بَعْضُكُمْ بَعْضًا أَيُحِبُّ أَحَدُكُمْ أَنْ يَأْكُلَ لَحْمَ أَخِيهِ مَيْتًا فَكَرِهْتُمُوهُ وَاتَّقُوا اللَّهَ إِنَّ اللَّهَ تَوَّابٌ رَحِيمٌ.

O you who have faith! Avoid much suspicion. Indeed some suspicions are sins. And do not spy on or backbite one another. Will any of you love to eat the flesh of his dead brother? You would hate it. And be wary of Allah; indeed Allah is all-clement, all-merciful. (49: 12)

Summary of Commentary:

In the above verse, God directly forbids man from three deeds that are the cause and effect of each other; first of all from suspicion, then from spying, and finally from backbiting. It is clear that suspicion makes man search for others' life and discover their secrets; and since everybody may have defects detected by the investigation, finding out that secret will cause backbiting.

Suspicion

In the above verse, man is explicitly forbidden from suspicion which is implicitly considered as an introduction for spying and backbiting, "O you who have faith! Avoid much suspicion. Indeed some suspicions are sins."

The interpretation of "much suspicion" is because the most suspicions of people are wrong suppositions about each other; therefore, the word "much" refers to this issue. It is also likely that the word "much" does not mean that most of the suspicions are bad, but that there are many bad suspicions, even if they are not much in comparison to the good ones. However, it seems the verse points to the first meaning.

It is noteworthy that after forbidding from suspicions, God explains why some of the suspicions are sins; this means the evil suspicions are of two kinds: some are true, and some are untrue. What is true is a sin, and since it is unclear which of the suspicions are true and untrue, one must avoid all bad suppositions to avoid untrue suspicions and sins.

Moreover, since suspicion about people's personal life is one of the means of spying, which leads to finding out their hidden defects followed by backbiting, the verse first forbids man from evil suspicions, then from spying finally from backbiting.

Spying

Spying means searching in people's personal life and affairs, often in undesirable and immoral cases. In fact, bad suspicion causes man to search for peoples' secrets motivated sometimes by other factors such as stinginess, envy, and narrow-mindedness.

To spy, as described above, is strictly forbidden in Islam. It causes social insecurity and is the source of all kinds of hostilities. If man is allowed to spy on others' privacy, he will make many people feel ashamed. Also, malice and hostility will be amplified in society, and this will make life a hell where all people will be tormented.

Of course, this moral and Islamic command never contradicts the necessity of the activities of intelligence agencies in an Islamic state because that relates to the individuals' private life, whereas this relates to the fate of the society and the prevention of the influence of foreign elements and conspiracy and destruction by them. With this explanation, we return to the Holy Qur'an.

This is the only verse of the Holy Qur'an that explicitly forbids man from spying. It is noteworthy that forbidding man from spying in verse 12 of Sura al-Ḥujurāt has no restriction which indicates the reverence of spying as a general rule. If it is allowed in certain circumstances and for more essential purposes, it will be an exception. The above verse and the importance of spying among Muslims were so clear that people also argued it in their relevant affairs.

Backbiting

The Holy Qur'an, in the verse discussed, considers backbiting more important than suspicion and spying because of an apparent reason, "Or backbite one another. Will any of you love to eat the flesh of his dead brother? You would hate it."

This simile, which constitutes a rational reason, expresses all the dimensions of backbiting and likens the backbitten man to a dead one, his religious relation to brotherhood, his honor to a part of his body, and backbiting to eating his flesh, a deed which every conscientious person, no matter how weak he is, is afraid of and would not like to do even in the worst conditions. This simile also refers to many other points: the backbitten man is like a dead one who has no power to defend himself and rushing on someone who cannot defend himself is the worst kind of unfair deeds.

Undoubtedly, eating the flesh of a dead body does not cause the health of the body and soul, but it is the source of all kinds of illnesses; so if the backbiting person quenches temporarily his grudge and jealousy by backbiting, certainly the same moral defects will be developed in his life. A backbiting man is a weak person without any courage to confront problems and therefore he rushes his dead brother.

Like a carcass-eating animal or man that spreads all kinds of microbial diseases, the backbiting man also paves the way of the proliferation of prostitution by talking about the sins and the hidden imperfections of his Muslim brothers.

Providing this example and its details, the Holy Qur'an stimulates the conscience and nature of man against this great sin. Maybe that is why it begins the sentence with a question to encourage him to respond, and that is why it highlights its effect stronger, it reads, "Will any of you love to eat the flesh of his dead brother?"

The verse also points to the cases when backbiting is permitted, such as pleading, eliminating oppression, consultation, and reconciliation between people which are the emergency cases when a man should backbite at its least extent.

However, here is a question. Throughout the world, we rarely encounter a man who eats the dead one's flesh, let alone his dead brother's; this is such a nasty deed that everyone avoids it. At the same time, backbiting is a common occurrence in all societies, one of the means of recreation and entertainment in meetings, where does this difference originate?

This apparently does not have any reason except that the prevalence of backbiting has decreased its nastiness among people.

Socialism and Isolationism

وَاعْتَصِمُواْ بِحَبْلِ اللهِ جَمِيعًا وَلاَ تَفَرَّقُواْ وَاذْكُرُواْ نِعْمَةَ اللهِ عَلَيْكُمْ إِذْ كُنتُمْ أَعْدَاء فَأَلَّفَ بَيْنَ قُلُوبِكُمْ فَأَصْبَحْتُم بِنِعْمَتِهِ إِخْوَانًا وَكُنتُمْ عَلَىَ شَفَا حُفْرَةٍ مِّنَ النَّارِ فَأَنقَذَكُم مِّنْهَا كَذَلِكَ يُبَيِّنُ اللهُ لَكُمْ آيَاتِهِ لَعَلَّكُمْ تَهْتَدُونَ.

Hold fast, all together, to Allah's cord, and do not be divided [into sects]. And remember Allah's blessing upon you when you were enemies, then He brought your hearts together, so you became brothers with His blessing. And you were on the brink of a pit of Fire, whereat He saved you from it. Thus does Allah clarify His signs for you so that you may be guided. (3: 103)

Summary of Commentary:

Inspired by the Book, the tradition, and reason researchers regard the principle of human beings' life as socialist and believe that a human is a social being who can achieve high goals, solve problems more efficiently, and achieve prosperity faster only context of the society. The scholars believe that separation and isolation are incompatible with man's nature or with Islam's teachings.

This verse invites people to "hold to Allah's cord" and "not to be divided [into sects]". What is meant by "Allah's cord" in the above verse? The commentators have different interpretations. It has been said in some of the narrations that by "Allah's cord" it means the Holy Qur'an that all people should hold it as the reason of unity. In some other traditions, "Allah's cord" means the Prophet's family. It turns out that all these refer to one fact, Allah's cord means a relationship to God that is obtained through the Qur'an, the Prophet and his family.

It is true that this verse discusses the friendship of Muslims with each other and avoiding hostility; but certainly, if human beings live in isolation, the friendship of all groups and holding Allah's cord will be meaningless. In the above verse, the Qur'an regards hostility as a tradition of the era of ignorance and calls friendship and affection as two of the characteristics of Islam. It reads, "When you were enemies, then He brought your hearts together, so you became brothers with His blessing." Regarding this verse and for more emphasize, God says, "And you were on the brink of a pit of Fire, whereat He saved you from it. Thus does Allah clarify His signs for you so that you may be guided."

It is also worth noting that Islam does not regard Muslims' relationship with each other as a friendship, but rather as a brotherhood which is the closest emotional relationship of two human beings to each other based on equality. Brothers can never be far away from each other and live unaware of their lives; they will surely be close to each other by this emotional bond.

Another critical point is that material life can never be the reason for unity, and it can never strengthen social connections. Instead it is always the source of conflict and controversy. People's demands are unlimited, whereas the material affairs are limited, which leads to disputes. However, Allah's cord and the relationship with God, which is a spiritual matter, can establish the best emotional relationship between human beings of all nations, races, languages and social groups.

Index

'

'Ajam., 109
'Alī, 89, 114
'Āllama Amini, 89
'Āllama Majlisi, 9
'Ibādallah, 90

A

Abrar, 90
Abū Hamzah al-Thumālī, 57
Abu Sa'id Khudrī, 46
Adam, 50, 64, 65
Ahl al-Bayt, 89
al-Ghadir, 89
al-jihad al-Akbar, 7, 8, 61
al-jihad al-Asghar, 7, 61
Allah's cord, 124, 125, 126
Amīr al-Mu'minīn 'Alī, 21, 26
Amir al-Mu'minān, 112, 114
Amr bil Ma'ruf, 16, 17

B

Balaam, 109
Beijing, 19
Biḥār al-Anwār, 8, 9, 10, 13, 26, 33, 36, 52, 90

C

China, 19
Christian, 109
Christian-Roman, 109
Christians, 21, 107

D

Divine Meditation, 24, 32, 33

E

Egypt, 73

F

Fakhr Razi, 88, 105
Fāṭimah Zahra, 89

G

Gabriel, 44

H

hadith, 9, 13, 26, 29, 33, 35, 39, 44, 46, 49, 51, 52, 58, 67, 79, 81, 85, 88, 89, 90, 93, 95, 99, 112, 114, 115, 117
hadiths, 37, 40, 104, 112
Hajj pilgrim, 43

Ḥ

Ḥasan, 26, 90

H

Hezbollah, 108
Hijaz, 101
Hūd, 26

Ḥ

Ḥusayn, 90

I

Iblīs, 64, 65
Ibrāhīm, 60
Imām 'Alī, 33, 37, 39, 46, 49, 52, 58, 65, 76, 79, 81, 93, 95, 117
Imām 'Alī ibn al- Ḥusayn, 10
Imām Ḥasan Al-Mujtabā, 26
Imām Riḍā, 26, 45
Imām Sādiq, 90
Imām Ṣādiq, 52, 91, 95, 99
Imām Sajjād, 31, 44, 57
Iran, 20

J

Jabr, 109
Jesus, 44, 107
jihad, 7, 8, 87, 93
Jihad, 7
Joseph, 82

K

Ka'ba, 101, 106
Kharijites, 21

khutbah al- Qāsi'ah, 65

L

Luqmān Hakim, 35

M

Majma' al-Bayan, 13, 46, 52, 88, 103
Majma' al-Bayān, 109, 110
Ma'rifat Allah, 50, 51
ma'rifat al-nafs, 49
Mary, 43, 44
Mary's infant, 44
Mecca, 101, 106, 118
Moses, 74, 98, 99
mu'āqaba, 24, 36, 37
mu'ātaba, 24, 36, 37
Mufradat, 46
Mufradāt, 67
Muhajirun, 108
Muhammad, 110
mu*hāsaba*, 36
Mu*hāsaba*, 24, 34, 35
Muraqaba, 24, 32, 33
mushārata, 24, 30, 31, 32, 33
Mushārata, 30

N

Nahj al-Balāghah, 37, 38
Nahrawān, 21
Nahy an al Munkar, 16
Nimrods, 74
Noah, 97, 98

P

Persian, 88
Pharaoh, 73, 74, 99
Pharaohs, 74, 99
Pledge, 24, 30
Prophets, 25, 77, 97
purification of souls, 2, 3
purification of the soul, 13, 47, 51

Q

Qarḍ al-Hasana, 115
Qaroun, 94, 95
Qurb-e-Elahi, 9, 78

R

Rāghib, 46, 67
remembrance, 30, 39, 53, 54, 55, 56, 57, 58, 60, 84

Remembrance, 53, 54, 56
Resurrection, 40, 60, 107
Rūḥ al-Qudus, 109

Ṣ

Ṣaḥīfa Sajjādiyya, 31

Ṣ

Ṣāliḥ, 26

S

Satan, 6, 14, 40, 58, 65, 91
self-accounting, 34, 35, 36
self-blaming, 36, 37
self-punishment, 24, 36, 37
self-reproach, 36, 37
Seyr-u Suluk, 9, 10, 78
Shari'a of Islam, 44
Shiite, 87, 89
shirk, 110
Sunni, 46, 87, 89

T

Tabarrā, 59
Tabrisi, 88, 103, 109, 110
Tafsir, 8, 13, 17, 19, 22, 23, 46, 51, 52, 85, 88, 93, 95, 105, 110, 119
Tafsir al-Mizan, 50
Tafsir 'Ithnā 'Ashari, 23
Tafsir Kabir, 105
Tafsir Qumi, 8
Tafsir Rūḥ al-Bayān, 22, 85, 110, 119
Taqiya, 77
Tawallā, 59
the Ansar, 108
the Battle of Aḥzāb, 60, 61
the Battle of the Tribes, 60
the Battle of Uhud, 103
the Christian, 21
the Day of Judgment, 14, 29, 35, 36
the Day of Reckoning, 35
The Day of Reckoning, 35
the Day of Resurrection, 14, 28, 29, 107
the Dharr world, 49
the Friday prayers, 43
the infallible Imāms, 38, 60
the Jews, 21
the Muhajirun, 108
the Prophet, 2, 12, 13, 14, 16, 25, 26, 31, 40, 46, 58, 60, 67, 71, 75, 77, 86, 87,

89, 93, 99, 101, 102, 103, 106, 109, 110, 115, 125
the Prophet Ibrāhīm, 77
the Prophets, 17, 77, 78
the Resurrection Day, 40

U

Uthman bin Talha, 106

Y

Yasar, 109
Yawm Al- Ḥisāb, 35
Yūsuf, 82, 83

www.ingramcontent.com/pod-product-compliance
Lightning Source LLC
Chambersburg PA
CBHW010707020526
44107CB00082B/2700